"At last! A much-needed book primarily an〈 consultant's continuing quest for personal a................................... for one's true inner self and outward for that self in relation to clients. I do strongly agree with the authors' basic thesis that we cannot expect our clients to embrace change unless we personally embrace it ourselves."

    —Bob Tannenbaum
        emeritus professor of the development of human systems,
        Anderson Graduate School of Management, UCLA,
        and recipient of Life Time Achievement Award from
        the National OD Network

"To become a psychotherapist one works on self awareness and understanding first. Psychotherapists are deeply involved with individual change in their work. Should those of us who work with change in organizations be any different? We need to be just as self-aware. Quade and Brown provide a highly useful way of helping us to do just that. Their simple but elegant model is the Tao of becoming an effective change agent."

    —W. Warner Burke
        professor of psychology and education,—Teachers College,
        Columbia University, and senior advisor, Pricewaterhouse Coopers

"Quade and Brown offer us one of the simplest, yet most powerful set of tools for doing the personal work required in conscious transformation. Every leader, change agent and member of a transforming organization needs to master this discipline as an accelerator of their changes, no matter how big or small. Better yet, apply it to every aspect of life!"

    —Linda Ackerman Anderson
        cofounder and principal, Being First, Inc. and coauthor of
        Beyond Change Management and *The Change Leader's Roadmap*

"The model described here provides many helpful guideposts, suggestions, and examples to help you operate from your core and be all you can be on your change consultant journey. The authors share many examples of the right questions to ask that stimulate and facilitate change in human systems of any size. This book is a real support and an 'upper'."

    —Dr. Lawrence L. Lippitt
        author, *Preferred Futuring: Envision the Future You Want*
        and Unleash the Energy to Get There

"Quade and Brown provide a well-grounded model on how to guide a consultants efforts through the potential hazards of organizational transformation. The material is well presented, with many examples, and is easy to follow and understand. Change is the most difficult subject any organization must deal with. Transformation takes leadership, and seasoned guidance. The guidelines provided by the authors provide that seasoned guidance. The material presented is not only well worthwhile for consultants, but management would be well served by mastering the tools provided by Quade and Brown."

—F. K. (Joe) Holtzman
retired, Oracle Corporation and
McDonnell Douglas/Boeing Corporation

Practicing Organization Development

**The Change Agent Series
for Groups and Organizations**

MISSION STATEMENT

The books in this series are intended to be cutting-edge, state-of-the-art, and innovative approaches to participative change in organizational settings. They are written for, and written by, organization development (OD) practitioners interested in new approaches to facilitating participative change. They are geared to providing both theory and advice on practical application.

SERIES EDITORS

**William J. Rothwell
Roland Sullivan
Kristine Quade**

EDITORIAL BOARD

**David Bradford
W. Warner Burke
Edith Whitfield Seashore
Robert Tannenbaum
Christopher G. Worley
Shaolin Zhang**

The Conscious Consultant

The Conscious Consultant

Mastering Change from the Inside Out

Kristine Quade
Renée M. Brown

**Forewords by Richard Beckhard
and Charles Seashore**

JOSSEY-BASS/PFEIFFER
A Wiley Company
www.pfeiffer.com

Practicing
Organization
Development

Published by

JOSSEY-BASS/PFEIFFER

A Wiley Company
989 Market Street
San Francisco, CA 94103-1741
415.433.1740; Fax 415.433.0499
800.274.4434; Fax 800.569.0443

www.pfeiffer.com

Jossey-Bass/Pfeiffer is a registered trademark of Jossey-Bass Inc., A Wiley Company.

ISBN: 0-7879-5880-8

Library of Congress Cataloging-in-Publication Data

Quade, Kristine, 1948-
  The conscious consultant : mastering change from the inside out
/ by Kristine Quade, Renee M. Brown.
    p. cm. — (The practicing organization development
series)
Includes bibliographical references and index.
  ISBN 0-7879-5880-8
  1. Consultants—Handbooks, manuals, etc. 2. Organizational
change—Handbooks, manuals, etc. I. Brown, Renee M., 1946- II.
Title. III. Series.
  HD69.C6 Q33 2002
  658.4'06—dc21

2001002025

Printed in the United States of America.

We at Jossey-Bass strive to use the most environmentally sensitive paper stocks available to us. Our publications are printed on acid-free recycled stock whenever possible, and our paper always meets or exceeds minimum GPO and EPA requirements.

Jossey-Bass/Pfeiffer is a registered trademark of Jossey-Bass Inc., A Wiley Company.

Acquiring Editor: Matthew Holt	Senior Production Editor: Dawn Kilgore
Director of Development: Kathleen Dolan Davies	Manufacturing Supervisor: Becky Carreño
Developmental Editor: Susan Rachmeler	Interior and Cover Design: Bruce Lundquist
Editor: Rebecca Taff	Illustrations: Richard Sheppard

Printing   10 9 8 7 6 5 4 3 2 1

Contents

Foreword
to the Series

ON 1967, Warren Bennis, Ed Schein, and I were faculty members of the Sloan School of Management at MIT. We decided to produce a series of paperback books that collectively would describe the state of the field of organization development (OD). Organization development as a field had been named by myself and several others from our pioneer change effort at General Mills in Minneapolis, Minnesota, some ten years earlier.

Today I define OD as "a systemic and systematic change effort, using behavioral science knowledge and skill, to transform the organization to a new state."

In any case, several books and many articles had been written, but there was no consensus on whether OD was a field of practice, an area of study, or a profession. We had not even established OD as a theory or even as a practice.

We decided that there was a need for something that would describe the state of OD. Our intention was to each write a book and also to recruit three other authors. After some searching, we found a young editor who had just joined the small publishing house of Addison-Wesley. We made contact, and the series was born. Our audience was to be human resource professionals who spent their time consulting with managers in their development through various small-group activities, such as team building. More than thirty books have been published in that series, and the series has had a life of its own. We just celebrated its thirtieth anniversary.

At last year's National OD Network Conference, I said that it was time for the OD profession to change and transform itself. Is that not what we change agents tell our clients to do? This new Jossey-Bass/Pfeiffer series will do just that. It can be seen as:

- A documentation of the re-invention of OD;

- An effort that will take us to the next level; and

- A practical effort to transfer to the world the theory and practice of leading-edge practitioners and theorists.

The books in this new series will thus prove to be valuable resources for change agents to keep current with the new and leading-edge ideas and practices.

May this very exciting change agent series be most creative and innovative. May it give our field a renewed burst of energy and awareness.

Richard Beckhard
Written on Labor Day weekend 1999 from my summer cabin near Bethel, Maine

Introduction to the Series

"We must become the change we want to see."

—*Mahatma Gandhi*

"We live in a moment of history where change is so speeded up that we begin to see the present only when it is already disappearing."

—*R. D. Laing*

WE CAN EXPECT MORE CHANGE to occur in our lifetimes than has occurred since the beginning of civilization over ten thousand years ago. *Practicing Organization Development: The Change Agent Series for Groups and Organizations* is a new series of books being launched to help those who must cope with or create change in organizational settings. That includes almost everyone.

The Current State of Organization Development

Our view of OD in this series is an optimistic one. We believe that OD is gaining favor as decision makers realize that a balance *must* be struck between the drivers of change and the people involved in it and affected by it. Although OD does have its disadvantages at a time characterized by quantum leap change, it remains prefer-able to such alternative approaches to change as coercion, persuasion, leadership change, and debate.[1] Organization development practitioners are reinventing their approaches, based on certain foundational roots of the field, in combination with emerging principles to ensure that OD will increasingly be recognized as a viable, important, and inherently participative approach to help people in organizations facilitate, anticipate, and manage change.

A Brief History of the Genesis of the OD Series

A few years ago, and as a direct result of the success of *Practicing Organization Development: A Guide for Practitioners* by Rothwell, Sullivan, and McLean, the publisher—feeling that OD was experiencing a rebirth of interest in the United States and in other nations—wanted to launch a new OD series. The goal of this new series was not to replace, or even compete directly with, the well-established Addison-Wesley OD Series (edited by Edgar Schein). Instead, as the editors saw it, this series would provide a means by which the most promising authors in OD whose voices had not previously been heard could share their ideas. The publisher enlisted the support of Bill Rothwell, Roland Sullivan, and Kristine Quade to turn the dream of a series into a reality.

This series was long in the making. After sharing many discussions with the publisher and circulating among themselves several draft descriptions of the series editorial guidelines, the editors were guests of Bob Tannenbaum, one of the field's founders, in Carmel, California, in February 1999 to discuss the series with a group of well-known OD practitioners interested in authoring books. Several especially supportive publisher representatives, including Matt Holt and Josh Blatter, were also present at that weekend-long meeting. It was an opportunity for diverse OD practitioners, representing many philosophical viewpoints, to come together to share their vision for a new book series. In a sense, this series represents an OD inter-vention in the OD field in that it is geared to bringing change to the field most closely associated with change management and facilitation.

---

[1]W. Rothwell, R. Sullivan, & G. McLean. (1995). Introduction (pp. 3–46). In W. Rothwell, R. Sullivan, & G. McLean, *Practicing Organization Development: A Guide for Consultants.* San Francisco, CA: Jossey-Bass/Pfeiffer.

What Distinguishes the Books in this Series

The books in this series are meant to be cutting-edge and state-of-the-art in their approach to OD. The goal of the series is to provide an outlet for proven authorities in OD who have not put their ideas into print or for up-and-coming writers in OD who have new, sometimes unorthodox, approaches that are stimulating and exciting. Some of the books in this series describe inspirational concepts that can lead to actionable change and purvey ideas so new that they are not fully developed.

Unique to this series is the cutting-edge emphasis, the immediate applicability, and the ease of transferability of the concepts. The aim of this series is nothing less than to reinvent, re-energize, and reinvigorate OD. In each book, we have also recommended that the author(s) provide:

- A research base of some kind, meaning new information derived from practice and/or systematic investigation and

- Practical tools, worksheets, case studies and other ready-to-go approaches that help the authors drag "theory" to "practice" to make these new, cutting-edge approaches more concrete.

Subject Matter That Will (and Will Not) Be Covered

The books in this series are varied in their approach, but they are united by their focus. All share an emphasis on organization development (OD). Hence, books in this series are about participative change efforts. They are not about such other popular topics as leadership, management development, consulting, group dynamics—unless those topics are treated in new, cutting-edge ways and are geared to OD practitioners.

This Book

As change agents, we are the instruments of our work. *The Conscious Consultant: Mastering Change from the Inside Out* helps consultants to understand that their self-knowledge and development is not isolated, but actually essential to their competence in guiding others in change. The idea that the change agent must practice personal change to be effective in guiding others in change becomes integrated at a new level. This book presents a simple and elegant new change model and helps the reader apply the change model to personal as well as client change. Explored are ten personal foundations crucial to the development of the consultant.

These foundations have a direct relationship with the quality of the consultant's client work.

This book will help consultants become profoundly skillful as change agents as they learn more about how to change who they are in a way that improves the outcome of client interventions. Examples, exercises and stories, some by leading practitioners, help consultants to do the following:

- Learn how to use a simple change model that can be applied to all kinds of change;

- Define and assess ten personal foundations;

- Understand what needs to be strengthened personally to facilitate phenomenal leadership in change;

- Learn seven dimensions of insightful questions that lead clients on a mutual quest within the change process;

- Make conscious agreements with self and clients; and

- Learn to look for what gets in the way of conscious change.

Series Website

For further information and resources about the books in this series and about the current and future practice of organization development, we encourage readers to visit the series website at *www.PracticingOD.Pfeiffer.com.*

William J. Rothwell
University Park, PA

Roland Sullivan
Deephaven, MN

Kristine Quade
Minnetonka, MN

Statement
of the Board

IT IS OUR PLEASURE TO PARTICIPATE in and influence the start up of *Practicing Organization Development: The Change Agent Series for Groups and Organizations.* The purpose of the series is to stimulate the profession and influence how OD is defined and practiced. This statement is intended to set the context for the series by addressing three important questions: (1) What is OD? (2) Is the OD profession at a crossroads? and (3) What is the purpose of this series?

What Is Organization Development?

We offer the following definition of OD to stimulate debate:

> Organization development is a system-wide and values-based collaborative process of applying behavioral science knowledge to the adaptive development, improvement, and reinforcement of such organizational features as the strategies, structures, processes, people, and cultures that lead to organization effectiveness.

The definition suggests that OD can be understood in terms of its several foci:

First, *OD is a system-wide process.* It works with whole systems. In the past, the bias has been toward working at the individual and group levels. More recently, the focus has shifted to organizations and multi-organization systems. We support that trend in general but honor and acknowledge the fact that the traditional focus on smaller systems is both legitimate and necessary.

Second, *OD is values-based.* Traditionally, OD has attempted to distinguish itself from other forms of planned change and applied behavioral science by promoting a set of humanistic values and by emphasizing the importance of personal growth as a key to its practice. Today, that focus is blurred and there is much debate about the value base underlying the practice of OD. We support a more formal and direct conversation about what these values are and how the field is related to them.

Third, *OD is collaborative.* Our first value commitment as OD practitioners is to bring about an inclusive, diverse workforce with a focus of integrating differences into a world-wide culture mentality.

Fourth, *OD is based on behavioral science knowledge.* Organization development should incorporate and apply knowledge from sociology, psychology, anthropology, technology, and economics toward the end of making systems more effective. We support the continued emphasis in OD on behavioral science knowledge and believe that OD practitioners should be widely read and comfortable with several of the disciplines.

Fifth, *OD is concerned with the adaptive development, improvement, and reinforcement of strategies, structures, processes, people, culture, and other features of organizational life.* This statement not only describes the organizational elements that are the target of change, but also describes the process by which effectiveness is increased. That is, OD works in a variety of areas, and it is focused on improving these areas. We believe that such a statement of process and content strongly implies that a key feature of OD is the transference of knowledge and skill to the system so that it is more able to handle and manage change in the future.

Sixth and finally, *OD is about improving organization effectiveness.* It is not just about making people happy; it is also concerned with meeting financial goals, improving productivity, and addressing stakeholder satisfaction. We believe that OD's future is closely tied to the incorporation of this value in its purpose and the demonstration of this objective in its practice.

Is the OD Profession at a Crossroads?

For years, OD professionals have said that OD is at a crossroads. From our perspective at the beginning of the new millennium, the field of organization development can be characterized by the following statements:

1. Practitioners today are torn. The professional organizations representing OD practitioners, including the OD Network, the OD Institute, the International OD Association, and the Academy of Management's OD and Change Division, are experiencing tremendous uncertainties in their purposes, practices, and relationships.

2. There are increasing calls for regulation/certification.

3. Many respected practitioners have suggested that people who profess to manage change are behind those who are creating it. Organization development practitioners should lead through influence rather than follow the lead of those who are sometimes coercive in their approach to change.

4. The field is defined by techniques.

5. The values that guide the field are unclear and ill-defined.

6. Too many people are practicing OD without any training in the field.

7. Practitioners are having difficulty figuring out how to market their services.

The situation suggests the following provocative questions:

- How can OD practitioners help formulate strategy, shape the strategy development process, contribute to the content of strategy, and drive how strategy will be implemented?

- How can OD practitioners encourage an open examination of the ways organizations are conceived and managed?

- How can OD focus on the drivers of change external to individuals, such as the external environment, business strategy, organization change, and culture change, as well as on the drivers of change internal to individuals, such as individual interpretations of culture, behavior, style, and mindset?

- How much should OD be part of the competencies of all leaders and how much should it be the sole domain of professionally trained, career-oriented OD practitioners?

What Is the Purpose of This Series?

This series is intended to provide current thinking about OD as a field and to provide practical approaches based on sound theory and research. It is targeted for full-time external or internal OD practitioners; top executives in charge of enterprise-wide change; and managers, HR practitioners, training and development professionals, and others who have responsibility for change in organizational and trans-organizational settings. At the same time, these books will be directed toward cutting-edge thinking and state-of-the-art approaches. In some cases, the ideas, approaches, or techniques described are still evolving, so the books are intended to open up dialogue.

We know that the books in this series will provide a leading forum for thought-provoking dialogue within the OD field.

About the Board Members

David Bradford is senior lecturer in organizational behavior at the Graduate School of Business, Stanford University, Palo Alto, California. He is co-author (with Allan R. Cohen) of *Managing for Excellence, Influence Without Authority*, and *POWER UP: Transforming Organizations Through Shared Leadership*.

W. Warner Burke is professor of psychology and education and chair of the Department of Organization and Leadership at Teachers College, Columbia University, New York, New York. His most recent publication is *Business Profiles of Climate Shifts: Profiles of Change Makers* (with William Trahant and Richard Koonce).

Edith Whitfield Seashore is organization consultant and co-founder (with Morley Segal) of AUNTL Masters Program in Organization Development. She is co-author of *What Did You Say?* and *The Art of Giving and Receiving Feedback* and co-editor of *The Promise of Diversity*.

Robert Tannenbaum is emeritus professor of development of human systems, Graduate School of Management, University of California, Los Angeles; recipient of Lifetime Achievement Award by the National OD Network. He has published numerous books, including *Human Systems Development* (with Newton Margulies and Fred Massarik).

Christopher G. Worley is director, MSOD Program, Pepperdine University, Malibu, California. He is co-author of *Organization Development and Change* (7th ed.), with Tom Cummings, and of *Integrated Strategic Change*, with David Hitchin and Walter Ross.

Shaolin Zhang is senior manager of organization development for Motorola (China) Electronics Ltd. He received his master's degree in American Studies from Beijing Foreign Studies University, Beijing, China, and holds a Ph.D. in sociology from York University, Toronto, Canada.

Foreword

ⓑECOMING A FULLY CONSCIOUS PRACTITIONER is a powerful challenge for interventionists of all persuasions. It is essential if we are to use our capacities to reflect on our experiences to form useful models and theories, which can, in turn, inform our work. Basing our practice on application of theory is difficult enough, as anyone can attest who consistently attends to walking his or her talk. Letting our experience inform our models may be a bigger challenge. Letting our models and theories evolve over time in parallel with our consulting experience demands an ability to articulate our own models, to reflect, and to gather reliable feedback on outcomes while managing oneself in the dynamic world of human systems. My father, an experimental psychologist, once said, "A major distinction between rats and people is that rats can learn from experience!" That somewhat exaggerated assertion frames the challenge for each of us who desires to become a conscious consultant in the improvement of human systems.

This book presents opportunity to engage in a dialogue with two active practitioners of our art who have organized their experiences along with reflections contributed by many of our colleagues. *The Conscious Consultant* outlines a framework that has proven helpful and can be a significant contribution for OD practitioners in two ways: (1) It can help us to consider how their framework might be adopted or adapted for our own use, and (2) it will serve as a catalyst for an inner dialogue that will lead us to become more articulate about models that work for each of us—models that can evolve in response to our own experiences and the experiences of our colleagues.

Consulting is a process in which "mistakes" are inevitable. Our competence at managing our world of feedback is critical. It is a multi-step process. It is important that we first work with clients and make our best judgments on a course of action. What we do next is what is critical—we pay attention to what has happened as a result of our effort. Some of our best work is what we do after we have "made the mistake." If we were surgeons, some of these mistakes would be extremely serious. Fortunately, our consultant work is rarely about life-and-death matters. It is more developmental. When we err, we generally do not put the life of our client in harm's way. However, it may be likely that we will find ourselves in harm's way if we do not systematically challenge our own values, strategies, styles, and theories. A recent *New Yorker* cartoon pictured two detectives looking down at the feet of a body (most of which is outside the frame of the cartoon) saying, "From the violent nature of the stab wounds, I would say it is probably a consultant." It is clearly in our own self-interest to follow Lewin's advice that there is nothing as practical as a good theory. And the theory we are talking about here is our own framework of beliefs and concepts.

Reading and understanding what these authors have to say motivates us to seek feedback on the different "screens" we use to illuminate our work. We know that, as professionals, we may in fact be inclined to help other people give and receive feedback—and at the same time neglect ways of inquiring about the viability of our own perspectives. This would include any models and implicit theories that help us link our perceptions to the world of actions.

The authors present a model of stages in the process of contracting through taking action that we can use to help us reflect on our own experiences. I particularly like their approach to the management of our own defenses as we deal with that feedback. Comparing one's own model with that of another person can be a shocking and confronting experience—one that can easily arouse our defenses. I once gave a presentation to an audience of physical scientists about the potential of groups in the teaching/learning process. At the end of the session, in which I thought I had made some quasi-brilliant points, one person approached me with the following feedback: "Charlie, your presentation was clear, you had an example for every point that you wanted to make, and you had an interesting and humorous anecdote to help us have a vivid picture of your points. BUT, you might want to remember this–something not worth doing is not worth doing well." Not all feedback comes that quickly, but it is easy to respond defensively. By managing my defenses, I was able to rethink, revise, and improve on the model and the logic of my argument.

Consistent revision of one's own theory is as important as learning the latest strategies of action. Konrad Lorenz said, "It is a good morning exercise for a research scientist to discard a pet hypothesis every day before breakfast. It keeps one young." This practice could be a great catalyst for OD consultants working on nourishing our use of self as scholar practitioners. It is one of the implications of the paradigms presented as the authors urge us to become more self-conscious about our beliefs about the process of planned change.

Becoming conscious is a long-term process as well as coming in short spurts. I received feedback this last summer from a colleague who compared my morning sunrise seminar presentation to a talk I had given in 1969. Letting feedback ripen for thirty-two years before delivering it may not be the ideal model, but it did turn out to be helpful in my understanding of the feedback about my current work. I was lucky that this colleague was present when I "published" each of my models and was enlightened that he shared some observations that helped me understand issues of substance as well as of style. It helped me stretch my "consciousness" regarding my approach to consultation and enabled us to go deeper into some ideas of mutual concern. I found the same effect in an appreciative reading of this book.

Expanding our conscious awareness requires a discipline and an openness to material that is out of awareness. Professionals in general are prone to overlook evidence that our assumptions about our impact may be quite deviant from what we intend. Our reticence about self-reflection may be most evident if we simply consider the feedback we withhold from our colleagues because we perceive them to be not ready, not accessible, or not interested in our ideas, especially if they conflict with their own favorite models. This can occur at any of the phases of OD work as we move through the spiral from the entry point of consultation to intervention and assessment of the outcomes of our actions.

I hope that all of us ask ourselves the question of how we can become more fully and deeply open to feedback—especially the reassessment and evolution of any favorite ways of carrying out our work. I have noticed that many of us are rather sensitive and even prickly about articulating and dialoguing with others about our preferred models of working, sometimes even taking refuge in the extreme intuitive space of not knowing why the things that work for us do turn out so well. On a more defensive note, we may be focused on using those parts of our selves that are rooted in unresolved issues from our past. We can use these strategies on "automatic pilot" without even knowing that we have been bypassing our conscious self and thus acting without choice.

Look around and ask yourself which colleagues fit your model of a "conscious consultant." What evidence do you use to make that judgment? What are they attending to and what is outside of their own awareness? How do they process information about their own style, ways of thinking, working, and interacting? More importantly, we can ask ourselves the same questions. How well do I manage the evolution of my own thinking? There is always room for expanding our areas of self that lie in the Blind or Unknown quadrants of the Johari Window. One way is to become better acquainted with and accepting of our own capacity for self-deception, illusion, and distortion. Looked at positively, we can embrace the notion that our own reality is in fact socially constructed. Our perceptions are one take on reality, but only one of many. This assumption can be particularly important as we do our diagnostic work in the human systems we are hoping to serve.

This book is about bringing the full self into our work. My colleague Cathy Royal is fond of saying that the nature of our work involves "looking out the window while we are looking in the mirror." Especially in emotionally charged situations such as diversity work, we will find situations where we will be resonating deeply within ourselves. We may have lots of difficulty dealing with skill and competence in those situations that stir up our unfinished business from early developmental years. Our models need to take into account how we know when we are working with our "vulnerable sides of self" and how we can pull back and pass the baton to partner with colleagues who at that moment may better serve the needs of the client.

So dig in. Engaging with the ideas in this book is an important way to challenge your own favorite ideas. Their process is a way of looking at our work and can help us develop a way for ourselves that is more conscious, more open to revision, and more humbling than settling for any of our perspectives that have become hardened and rigid over time. Expanding our conscious use of self may well be the best avenue to increase our own competence while contributing to the evolution of our field. Indeed, it may be the key element in continual self-differentiation over the entire life span that was envisioned by Jung.

Charles Seashore
Fielding Institute
July 2001

We dedicate this book to the
founders of the OD field, who so
generously gave us our foundation,
and to the visionaries of the OD field,
who wholeheartedly lead us into
the future.

Acknowledgments

ON THE TRUE SPIRIT of the organization development community, we received valuable contributions from those listed below. Each story and quote was provided as a means of helping others to understand the complexities of consciousness.

Geoff Bellman lives in Seattle and has consulted to large organizations for thirty-five years, including Verizon, BP-Amoco, Boeing, and the EPA. He has written five books: *Getting Things Done When You Are Not in Charge; The Consultant's Calling; Your Signature Path: Gaining New Perspectives on Life and Work; The Beauty of the Beast: Breathing New Life into Organizations;* and *The Collaborative Leader.*

Barbara Benedict Bunker is a professor of psychology at the University of Buffalo and a partner in the Portsmouth Consulting Group. She has taught executive development programs at Columbia, Pepperdine, and the Harvard Graduate School of Education. She has co-authored (with Billie Alban) *Large Group Interventions: Engaging the Whole System for Rapid Change.*

Kathy Dannemiller is the originator of the Whole-Scale Change Model, which started the 1980s movement toward large group interventions. She is the co-author of *Whole-Scale Change: Unleashing the Magic in Organizations* and the accompanying workbook, *Whole-Scale Change: The Tool Kit.*

Jim Earley is a pioneer in the field of coaching and the president of his own firm, Pathfinder Coaching, in Minneapolis, Minnesota. He is a certified Master Coach and the president of the Minnesota Coaches Association. He continues to provide creative leadership to the field of coaching.

Ken Hultman, Ed.D, is an independent organization development consultant, trainer, and coach. He holds a doctorate in counseling psychology from Rutgers University. He is the author of *Making Change Irresistible* and *Balancing Individual and Organizational Values.*

Robert "Jake" Jacobs has drawn from his extensive consulting experiences to write *Real Time Strategic Change,* a practical book and approach that leads to rapid and sustainable organization change. He has also co-authored a chapter in *Collaborating for Change* and written numerous articles on what it takes to implement fast and lasting change.

Kathy Joyce has been an internal consultant with the *Los Angeles Times* and Allied Signal. She currently serves as the Vice President of Human Resources for the *St. Louis Post Dispatch* and is a corporate officer with Pulitzer Corporation.

Kim Marshall is the principal of InnerCompass Coaching, a Minneapolis-based coaching practice. She helps personal and professional development clients from around the United States to reconnect with passion and to focus on what matters most.

Joan McIntosh is a Minneapolis-based consultant, coach, and trainer specializing in strengthening individual and team performance using groupware and graphics tools.

Alexandra Merrill has thirty-five years of experience in building women's communities in the United States and overseas. She developed Women's Way and has led several Women's Leadership Collaborations with Joyce Weir. Her primary teaching revolves around strengthening the practice of female authority in women in leadership positions.

Phil Mix is an organizational consultant based in the United Kingdom. His principal interest is risk taking by organizational leaders to maximize the potential of people and to reduce their excessive dependence on hierarchy. His recent clients include Shell (in the UK, the Netherlands, Malaysia, and Nigeria), Cable & Wireless, DHL, and the Bank of England.

Peter Norlin, Ph.D., has spent over twenty-five years as a leader-consultant in the human systems development profession, most recently as a principal in Green-Leaf Associates, Ann Arbor, Michigan, a consulting firm that assists executives and senior managers to embody leadership, to craft and guide effective change at all levels of the organization, and to use the power of collaboration to increase work spirit and business success.

Edie Seashore, an organization consultant, is past president of the NTL Institute and is the co-founder (with Morley Segal) of the AUNTL Masters Program in Organization Development. She is the co-author (with Charles Seashore and Jerry Weinberg) of *What Did You Say? The Art of Giving and Receiving Feedback* and co-editor of *The Promise of Diversity.*

Margaret Seidler has served as an internal consultant for a major electric and gas utility in South Carolina and for the largest county seat in Minnesota. Additionally, her work as an external consultant has included major projects for both The Atlanta Consulting Group and Community Works of North Carolina.

Ken Shepard specializes in strategy formulation, organization design, and strategy implementation. He is a principal with the Canadian Centre for Leadership and Strategy. He founded the management of change program at the Niagara Institute and directed it for a decade. His practice is largely based on requisite organization concepts developed by Elliott Jaques.

Robert Terry, Ph.D., is president of The Terry Group, a leadership design firm that constructs and delivers unique, long-term, intense, and playful leadership programs for all kinds of organizations. Dr. Terry is also an executive advisor and mentor, public speaker, and peer coach to leadership educators

Jane Magruder Watkins is a former Chair of the Board of the NTL Institute for Applied Behavioral Sciences. She is one of the pioneers in using the Appreciative Inquiry approach in the field of organization development and is the co-author (with Bernard Mohr) of *Appreciative Inquiry: Change at the Speed of Imagination.* She has more than thirty years of experience in the field and has worked in over fifty countries around the globe.

Michael Welp, Ph.D., leads EqualVoice, a consulting firm that helps organizations build lasting collaborative environments by providing tools for conflict resolution, learning, and change. He focuses on diversity as a source of transformation and unification. He is the recipient of the Minnesota ODN Practitioner of the Year Award for 2000.

Christopher G. Worley, Ph.D., is the director of the MSOD Program at Pepperdine University. He is co-author of *Organization Development and Change,* 7th ed. (with Tom Cummings) and of *Integrated Strategic Change* (with David Hitchin and Walter Ross).

We gratefully thank the following people:

- Donna Taylor, for her years of experience with change. Her excellent teachings guided our change model.

- Shannon Elmer, who carried the literary research burden and kept telling us we were onto something!

- Michael O'Neal met every deadline, sometimes working well past midnight to help us edit our work, making the chapters flow within each other and hang together as a unit.

- Susan Rachmeler of Jossey-Bass/Pfeiffer, who provided the exceptional supervision of the editing of our work.

- The Practicing OD Series editors, Dr. William Rothwell and Roland Sullivan, who gave us feedback and encouraged us throughout the process.

- Our clients and students, who helped to give life to the material through their own interpretations.

- Our first-draft readers: Michael Welp, Margaret Seidler, Joan McIntosh, Wendy Suter, Jane Giacobassi, Lynn DiEuliis, Denise Templeton, Dan Barr, Lori Keenan, Ken Brown, Kent Hann, and Darlene Goertz.

- Jim Earley, Sandra Giese, Eric Wickiser, and Julie Theobald—dedicated members of the consulting class—for helping this material take shape through their practice and support.

- The members of the Minnesota Organization Development Network who encourage this work. It is the view of peers that is the most helpful and challenging.

A special "thank you" goes to our husbands:

Ken Brown, who gave wonderful feedback and perspective throughout this process. Even though he is currently writing a novel and working full-time, he took up the slack at home and was 100 percent supportive.

Kent Hann, who supported and encouraged the writing of this book through patience, humor, and helpful perspectives when they were needed most. His critical contribution came at a time when he was also starting a new and fast-growing business.

These great guys supported us when we went on a seven-day cruise to the western Caribbean in order to write (and write we did!) and are still patiently waiting for their vacations!

Additionally, Renée would like to thank the following people:

- My daughter, Larina Ann Brown, for her love, enthusiasm and encouragement.

- My son, Randon Luke Brown, for his support, kindness, and help throughout this process.

- My in-laws, Richard and Doris Brown, who supported me wholeheartedly, as they always have.

- My friends, all of whom were interested, encouraging, and supportive. I am blessed to have them in my life.

Additionally, Kristine would like to thank the following people:

- My daughters, Emily Kister and Danielle Leggett, who continue to remind me of the exceptional nature of talented, young women.

- Joan Ungar, for her support and encouragement.

- My family and friends who formed the tight web of caring and concern as I wrote and lived the journey of this work from development to completion.

Introduction

THE CONSCIOUS CONSULTANT: *Mastering Change from the Inside Out* is written for organization development (OD) consultants who want to develop as individuals and serve their clients consciously.

We wrote this book because we felt that the field of organization development needed a deeper examination of how consultants' personal attributes impact the outcomes achieved with their clients. This book, which examines the topics of consciousness, change, and personal and professional development, may guide a consultant to begin a personal change process or help those already in the process of practicing personal change. This book shows consultants how to connect their personal work with the work they do with clients.

A *conscious* consultant is a person who is aware of who he or she is on the inside, as well as aware of who others are. The conscious consultant is a developed person, aware of her or his own timing, current state, and knowledge, and having a similar awareness of the client. The conscious consultant makes conscious choices in a thoughtful and wholehearted manner, practicing wisdom. The conscious consultant is aware of how his or her behavior and choices are impacting the client. Conversely, the *unconscious* consultant chooses reactively, without including all of the available knowledge.

The field of organization development is consumed with the complexities of rapid change playing out on a global level. It seems that every intervention requires more knowledge and adaptability than the one before. Mergers, acquisitions, and alliances are the norm. Working across functions and at a global and multi-cultural level increases the complexity. And what does that mean for the consultants? It means that *we* must expand personally and develop our selves to meet these challenges.

How This Book Is Organized

The Active Change Model that is presented in Chapter 1 can be used for any kind of change. It works with tiny or huge changes, personal or organization change. It is simple and user-friendly. The steps in the model are Perceive, Describe, Accept, Question, Act, and Change. We use the model in this book as a tool for personal change, as this is the beginning of mastering change from the inside out.

In Chapter 2, we examine the first three steps of the model and describe a system for consultants to become aware of their personal state in terms of ten Personal Foundations. The condition of either strength or weakness within each of these foundations is directly correlated to who we are and how we perform with our clients. The exercise at the end of this chapter helps readers to not only understand the condition of their Personal Foundations but also to create Foundation Development Plans as a step toward mastering change from the inside out.

Chapter 3 applies the Personal Foundations to client interactions. A consultant's awareness of how his or her Personal Foundations impact clients helps the consultant to make conscious choices for professional and personal change. The exercise at the end of this chapter helps the reader to expand on the Foundation Development Plan to include more aspects of professional work.

Chapter 4 explores the fourth step of the Active Change Model: Questions. We have developed seven essential dimensions that help us to understand the intricacies of good questions. These are explored in depth so consultants can further their skill in asking conscious and crucial questions.

Chapter 5 explores the fifth step of the model—Act—and how making conscious agreements with ourselves influences the kind of professional work that we do. In addition, we explore how the agreements we have with ourselves impact our agreements with clients.

Chapter 6 helps us to understand how what happens during our client work can be an opportunity for consciousness and growth. The concepts of *roadblocks to consciousness* and *triggers* and how to work with them are explored. We also look at planning for what usually happens during interventions.

Chapter 7 is an applications chapter. We present five stories of how other consultants have worked their own conscious change process.

Our Story

Kristine met Renée as a professional coach in 1993, and this coaching relationship has blossomed into a joint professional organization development practice. We share a lifelong interest and commitment to becoming conscious, wise, and mature human beings. Our forty years of collective experience reflects our deep interest and commitment to helping others. Renée's experience has been focused on individual coaching and teaching, while Kristine's has been focused on facilitating team and large, systemic, organization change. The idea for this book developed from a class that Renée was teaching for organization development consultants about self-development and consciousness as it applied to the consultants' professional work. Kristine and Renée developed a seminar, which they jointly presented until this book became a better venue for helping consultants in their life and practice. Many individuals have reported life-changing results from the use of this material.

While we were writing this book, each step along the way was accompanied by our own personal growth in working with the material. We applied the Active Change Model to ourselves and worked on strengthening the condition of our Personal Foundations. We each came up against our own blocks, triggers, projections, and general unconscious material.

We approached this book as a way of sharing what we have learned from our own journey in consciousness. We know that you will encounter new awareness of the condition of your Personal Foundations and become more conscious in the choices you make with your practice and with your clients.

Each of the chapters contains exercises that are designed to assist the reader in going deeper with the material. These exercises are an outcome of the work that we have done with clients, who have achieved profound results by taking the time to "dig into themselves."

Because stories are such a powerful way of learning, we have included numerous stories throughout this book, some anonymous and some provided by wonderful colleagues who were generous enough to share their perspectives on their lives' journeys in order to aid in the understanding of the material. To them we owe an eternal gratitude for the gift they have provided.

Throughout this book, we have generally avoided the word "you" to define the reader. We, as the authors, chose to refer to our readers in the inclusive pronoun of "we" instead of "you." We chose this approach because we felt that in most instances we were speaking about consultants and humanity in general terms. We did not want to presume that any of the text is necessarily true for every individual reader.

The Conscious
Consultant

1

Practicing Active Change

The Nature of Change

Change: It's here. Whether we like it or not, it's the nature of life on earth. We could call change a natural law, a kind of force that affects everything without exception. Wherever we look, we see that everything and everyone is in constant change. From a human standpoint, sometimes that change is wonderful and welcome, sometimes terrible and repugnant. But change is happening, constantly.

As humans we have a choice about how we relate to change. We can engage with change in a conscious, active way, or we can respond reactively. *Active* change is when we choose the best action possible from a multitude of options. We practice being conscious of the whole situation, and our awareness of possibilities is expanded. *Reactive* change is when we don't really choose what to do but act based on our unconscious. "They made me do it—I had no choice!" is reactive change. It happens when we are not aware of the choices we could make, often ending up doing the same thing we have always done, regardless of whether it works or not.

Active change involves a series of conscious, participative steps. When we understand how conscious change happens and the steps involved, we can practice it in a deliberate and intentional way. As we become skilled in the process, we can make the most of each step, resulting in change that is self-directed and strongly rooted.

The Active Change Model

From our experience as consultants and as individuals practicing personal change, as well as from our experience learning from other OD consultants and teachers, we have identified six steps that are involved in all conscious change. We call this six-step process the Active Change Model. It is simple yet elegant and can be used for any kind of change. It is like the paddle for a whitewater raft that makes it possible to navigate raging waters successfully. The paddle works in any kind of water, at any time. Its design might be adapted, but the principle stays the same. In the same way, the Active Change Model is a tool that can effectively guide us through the raging waters of change.

The Active Change Model goes deep into the structure of conscious change. There are many other change models—for example, those by Lewin (1958), Lippitt and Lippitt (1986), Beckhard (1969), French and Bell (1969), Dannemiller (1990), and so forth—but we believe this model is more fundamental than any other. The steps of the Active Change Model are implicit in each of the other models, but no other includes all of the steps specifically, and most don't mention any of the steps. This model can be found as the structural foundation of all conscious change.

However, just as the paddle of a whitewater raft must be consciously and actively applied to be useful, so must this model. Other models are designed for client interventions and can be extremely useful when the intervention follows the expected pattern. Today, however, reinvention is what is current in the business world. Using the Active Change Model as a guide, consultants can custom design their interventions each time.

The authors have a combined total of nearly forty years of practice in the OD field and even more years of commitment to a path of personal change and developing consciousness. During all of this time, we have had a particular interest in how people change. We have studied and practiced various change models and methods, but none seemed to work for every kind of change. This suggested that there had to be something more to conscious change than was being talked about.

Along the way we met Donna Taylor, an exceptional teacher of methods for personal growth. Her model for change is Acceptance, Responsibility, Control (of the issue), and then Change. We found this model to be effective and have used it personally and professionally, as well as taught it to others. Our model has evolved from hers, revising and expanding on it as we continued to experiment and learn what worked for ourselves and others.

The Active Change Model has now been used extensively over a period of many years, both in our personal change journeys and in our consulting practices, where we applied it as change agents with individuals, groups, and organizations. The model works. It is simple to learn and simple to use. Our clients have noticed that, with practice, it becomes smoothly integrated into the way they change themselves and help others to do so as well.

The process of active change includes six steps. Every active change involves all of these steps in sequential order. A major change may include hundreds or even thousands of complete cycles of these steps. The steps in the model are described below and shown graphically in Figure 1.1.

- *Perceive:* We become aware of something—a situation, person, place, thing, sensation, and so forth.

- *Describe:* We describe what we have perceived fully, using words.

- *Accept:* We accept what we have perceived and described. We make peace with the fact that what we perceive does exist as it is—that regardless of how we feel about it, it is the way it is.

- *Question:* We become a seeker embarking on a quest to investigate all the aspects and possibilities of the situation that we can discover. We use questions as a tool to dig for treasure. Our questions bring answers.

- *Act:* We put the answers to use by doing something different.

- *Change:* When a new action is taken, we have a different experience. This is change. This gives us something new to Perceive, Describe, Accept, Question, and Act on, which brings Change. This process can take place over and over again.

Figure 1.1. The Active Change Model

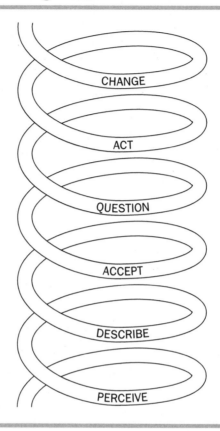

CHANGE

ACT

QUESTION

ACCEPT

DESCRIBE

PERCEIVE

Here is a simple example. I walk down the sidewalk. I *perceive* something different ahead. I *describe* the perception: There's a puddle on the sidewalk. Puddles consist of water. If I step in the puddle, my shoes will get wet. I don't want my shoes to get wet. I *accept* the situation: The puddle in this sidewalk is a fact. Even though it may annoy me, I don't argue with it—I accept it. I ask a *question*: What should I do to keep my shoes dry? I find an answer: Step around the puddle. I *act*: When I come to the puddle, I *change* my course and step around it. Now I face a new stretch of the sidewalk.

Let's look at each of the steps of the Active Change Model in more detail.

Perceive

"Lou," an internal consultant who works in a large state agency, shared his story with us:

> *"During successive meetings, I noticed that when I presented my ideas to the group, my supervisor took on defensive body language and criticized my ideas."*

In order for us to make a conscious, active change, we must first *perceive* what is happening. The perception may be about myself. It may involve the external, physical world. It may be about someone else's behavior. The situation will still exist, whether we are aware of it or not, but if we aren't aware, we won't be able to respond consciously. Change will still happen; if we try to ignore it, hoping it will go away, the situation may continue to deteriorate, or change might sneak up on and surprise us. We will be affected by the change, but we will have no part in moving the change in the direction we want. For this to happen, we need to see clearly what is going on. This may sound simple, but it is not necessarily easily done.

As humans, we are swimming in a vast ocean of information, both seen and unseen. We are only aware of a tiny fraction of that ocean, even though we are immersed in it. There is much that is present that we don't perceive on a conscious level. Some people are more aware than others. They have developed their ability to perceive and remain aware of more of the world within and around them. But all of us can learn to expand our perceptions to include more of what is happening.

At the heart of expanding our awareness is the practice of changing ourselves into more fully developed human beings. This involves change. We practice conscious, active change of ourselves. When we do this, the amount of what we perceive inside and outside of us multiplies.

As we practice change in ourselves, we may notice that we have *blocks.* Each of us has our own unique perspective from which we view our world. We all have our own blind spots and distortions. These blocks are patterns that we change only by using a conscious strategy. Forewarned of them, we can prepare ourselves to face and surmount them. Studying our blocks is like studying the enemy—if we know them well, we stand a chance of winning.

> *Lou wondered: "How objective am I? Am I having issues with authority figures? Am I projecting my dad onto my supervisor? Am I struggling for control?" Lou searched to find ways that his perception might not be accurate or complete.*

The most basic forms of blocking are *denial, attachment, mindset,* and *projection.* *Denial* is common in humans and (of course) in their organizations. Denial is when something is happening, but we refuse to acknowledge it. Kotter (1996) states that our belief that we face enough challenges without adding more, combined with our natural tendency to avoid bringing more work on ourselves, leads us to ignore evidence of a large problem if we can get away with it. Naturally, when this happens, *perceiving* what is happening is not on the horizon. This is compounded and made more dangerous when we deny that denial exists!

As consultants, we have found that, if in every situation we assume that important aspects of reality are being denied, we can plan for that denial. If no denial is present—so much the better. But if we assume that denial is present and plan reality checks along the way, we are much more likely to achieve functional and appropriate change without being blindsided by something significant that hasn't been included.

Another common block to accurate perception is *attachment.* We might have a strong attachment to things or people being a certain way. Usually, we become attached to an outcome because we believe it is the most comfortable, safe, or "right" way. If we find our selves engaged in rigid, insistent thinking, we might suspect that we are attached in some way. This is when we may have "tunnel vision" or "blinders" on. When we realize that we are safer with fuller perception, we may choose to let attachments go.

The *mindset* through which we perceive can further cloud our perceptions. It involves our belief systems about the way things work and how life is. Our mindset can determine what we expect to see and, therefore, what we do see. Here, self-knowledge is important. If we are aware of our mindset, we can know the ways in which we are likely to unconsciously limit our perceptions. Then we can learn to compensate or to open our mindset to become more accurate in our perceiving.

Similarly, we may *project* an image of someone onto another person. When we do this, we do not perceive the other person as he or she is but rather as the projected image of someone else. This someone else is often our own self. Or it might be someone from our past that we are still emotionally charged about. Usually, we project our own movie onto another individual when we are reminded of a past event or a part of our own self that we have not resolved.

When Lou asked the questions about how his own blocks might be distorting what he perceived, he risked receiving an unpleasant answer. He said, "I want to be effective and serve my team the best way I can, so I need to know all I can about what is going on."

Chris Argyris (1962) writes that individuals will deny or distort behaviors to which they cannot easily relate because they perceive those behaviors as a threat to themselves. What we find out may well make us uncomfortable, cause pain, or push us into action we would rather not take. To avoid this experience, we unconsciously distort and limit our perception of what is really happening, not realizing that this eventually results in more pain. Ultimately, we must decide how we wish to live. Comfortable in our delusions? Or, if necessary, uncomfortable with our truth? If we want to free ourselves from blocks and distortions, we need to become more interested in consciousness than in comfort. This requires courage.

How accurately we perceive will determine how well our active change process works. But the process itself will help us find what we need to know to integrate our change fully. We may cycle through the Active Change Model process many times as our perceptions become more accurate. As we overcome our tendency to block perception through denial, attachment, mindset, and projection, cycles of the active change process will go deeper and increase in impact.

Describe

First we *Perceive,* then we *Describe.* These two steps are so close together that they may seem inseparable, but they are distinct. To perceive is to have consciousness of something; to describe is to name what that something is.

When we describe something, we bring language to a perception. Language is how we make sense out of the world. Through the process of describing something, we become more conscious of what we are perceiving. For instance, we may feel air blowing on our face. We might say to ourselves, "The feeling I have is air blowing on my face. It's the wind." Now imagine that we have no words for air, wind, blow, or face. With language, we can describe our perceptions, and this activity makes it possible for us to perceive even more. With language we can ask questions that carry us deeper. "What is wind? What is air? Why does it move? If I can't see it, why does my face feel it?" The questions lead us to further knowledge and the possibility of more change. This comes from the power of naming, which is what it means to describe.

> *Lou noticed that the behavior of his supervisor was different toward him than toward others. He watched carefully and described to himself what was going on.*

Besides his supervisor's defensive body language and criticism of Lou's ideas,
Lou noticed other things. He realized that his supervisor looked for opinions from
people who were inclined to agree with his own ideas. The more fully Lou
described what was happening, the more he noticed.

We use the phrase "now that you mention it" when someone describes something we already know semi-consciously but haven't named. Describing what is in the periphery of our awareness expands our experience, gives us more information, and multiplies the choices we can make.

This naming of what is happening is a fundamental human activity that helps us feel real and connected. Imagine sitting at night in a room with a group of people. Suddenly the lights go out. No one comments on it, and everyone continues on as if nothing has happened. Everyone knows that the lights went out. So why would anyone need to remark on it? Yet, until someone says, "What happened to the lights?" we are tense. Why? Because we don't feel connected until we know we are sharing the same experience.

This is an example of describing to others, but we also need to describe to ourselves. This involves naming where we are right now. It's like knowing the names of the streets where we are standing and then finding where we are on a map. First we name what is happening; then we can locate ourselves on our inner map. Awareness of emotions offers a good example of this. We may perceive that we are having a feeling. When we name that feeling as an emotion, and then the particular emotion that we are experiencing, we can know where we are on the map. Then we can decide what to do next. "I'm feeling something" won't give us enough of a description to help us move on.

Naturally, Lou had some of his own feelings about these events. He said, "I was
really angry with him [the supervisor]. How could he behave like that? What a
child! And so unprofessional. Even though I had real evidence to back up my
ideas, he would pick them apart with anecdotes. My ideas are good! What a
waste." In order to minimize his own feelings of anger, Lou could have said to
himself, "It's OK; I understand." But that would have been inaccurate and would
have kept him from choosing what to do from where he actually was. Acknowl-
edging messy feelings is risky business, but he chose to do it anyway.

When we describe what we perceive, we are making a statement to ourselves or to others. Again, this involves risk. It means that we are exposing ourselves. It takes courage to describe our perceptions clearly and succinctly in a way that others can understand. And it takes courage to be honest in our descriptions, both to others and to ourselves.

The ability to describe clearly is not something we are born with. It's an acquired skill that we integrate into our habitual practice of consciousness. We can develop this ability by regularly looking around us with a fresh, open attitude and then describing our surroundings in detail. We can do the same thing as we observe an event or interaction. This can take just a few seconds or several minutes. What happens is that we open up more inside and feel more fully connected with our surroundings. This is one technique for becoming more conscious.

Some things that get in the way of clearly describing are poor language skills, lack of knowledge, and lack of self-confidence. Like most blocks, these can be remedied with practice and effort, using the Active Change Model.

Accept

We are what we are. Other people are what they are. Events happen as they do. These things are what they are and remain what they are, regardless of our opinions. Our opinions of whether or not something *should* be the way it already is are irrelevant to the fundamental reality of the situation. The opinions we hold may be relevant to us, but they do not change the way things are.

When we accept what is for what it is, we are not arguing about whether or not something *should* have happened. When we accept ourselves, we are not harassing ourselves about what we should or could have done differently. When we accept others for who they already are, we are not arguing about how they should be different.

Practicing acceptance does not mean giving up discernment. In accepting what is actually the case, we can see that certain actions have certain results. Some of the results are desirable, some not. Acceptance of the way things are enables us to perceive and describe more accurately.

Acceptance also does not mean we can't like it or dislike it. It does not mean that we give up any ideas of change. On the contrary, when we are able to accept, we are able to change in a conscious way. We are functioning in present time, and we can perceive and describe more fully. We can ask, "What do I need to do now?" Without acceptance, we are in reaction. We are busy saying, "This can't be happening. It must be someone's fault. Why me?"

Actually, Lou was very angry about his supervisor's behavior. He felt blocked in meetings and was frustrated all around: "Finally I decided to just let go. I still felt that my supervisor was a jerk, but I realized that the meetings were going to continue to be the way they had been. Since I was tired of feeling criticized, I no longer shared my ideas at the meetings." Lou had accepted the meetings for what they were and had moved on to new behavior. He felt that, under the circumstances, he was making the best choice available to him. He realized and accepted the fact that his clients and colleagues needed and wanted his help. He decided to build stronger connections with his team. But he still judged his supervisor.

Judging is what we are doing when we are *not* accepting. Judgment is when we make a determination that something or someone is right or wrong for being the way it is. We are saying that something that already is should not exist as it does. Or we are saying that something is right just as it is, and that anything different is wrong.

When we indulge in judgment, we may find ourselves entangled in a never-ending struggle for control. Rather than changing in a conscious and active way, we attempt to simply dictate our selves into being different. If we could change in this way, we would all be "perfect" by now. Or we might attempt to control other people or the outcome of events, usually by manipulation or attempted mental will power, which may be successful temporarily. Regardless of the evidence that we cannot actually control these things into changing, we still imagine it's possible and attempt to do so. These attempts will have an effect, but it is a reactive change.

Question

With accurate perception, description, and acceptance, we are prepared to embark on a *quest* of discovery as we take on the role of seeker. A seeker has an attitude of curiosity, openness, and courage. This attitude brings us to generate challenging, creative, and useful questions. When we are seekers, we want to find answers to our questions more than we want comfort.

The *Question* Stage of the Active Change Model is crucial to the whole change cycle. Asking good questions is a powerful skill. It is so important that a later chapter is devoted to it. Here, we will discuss the basics and leave the rest to later.

A good question is one that leads us to an answer that we need. A good question is clearly articulated and clearly states what we are seeking. And when we cannot think of a good question, any question will do. Questions (and the resulting answers) stimulate us to ask more questions. This questioning cycle can go on endlessly, because there is no limit on the number of possible questions.

Questions Lou asked included the following:

- *"I want to contribute and be effective at my work. Even though I'm not effective at the meetings, what other ways are available to me?"*
- *"How does my supervisor behave outside of meetings?"*
- *"How do other people in the office treat me?"*
- *"How do they respond to my ideas?"*
- *"What can I do that might be more helpful and functional?"*
- *"How am I contributing to my supervisor's behavior?"*

Lou took a risk when he asked these questions. He opened himself up to some answers that might have been unpleasant. There are danger zones in working with questions. Sometimes we only pretend to seek while getting stuck in patterns that stop us from moving forward. Sometimes we become attached to a particular, preconceived answer. Sometimes we feel compelled to find an answer right away, so we snatch the first easy one that comes along and run with it. When we do any of these, we are reacting and controlling, not searching. These behaviors lead to reactive change, and we find ourselves entrusting our fate to luck. The question step of the active change model involves strong skills, self-awareness, and courage.

Act

When we ask questions, we receive answers. When we receive answers, we choose how we will respond, which is to act. When we act, we decide how we will use an answer and then actually do something different based on the new information. We are creating, choosing, and doing something new. This action might be a physical action or a shift inside our selves. A shift inside of our selves is an internal action.

An internal action would go like this: We receive an answer to our question → The answer brings us a new revelation → The new revelation is a new perception → We describe it and accept it → We ask a new question → A new question is an action → A new question is also a change → We have a new revelation → and so on. This might be one of a series of internal cycles.

In the context of the Active Change Model, this internal change must eventually be physically acted on for it to be complete. This means that we not only think differently but act differently. Some may argue this point, but we feel that change is not complete until a physical action that is different is actually undertaken. What is only in our minds is just theory. We can run in endless mind loops. When we experiment in the physical laboratory of our lives, we test the theory. The test will have an observable result. This is the actual change.

> *Lou received lots of answers on his journey. During his investigation, he realized that his clients and colleagues appreciated his support and were open to his ideas. He said, "I realized that I brought my ideas to the meetings without sharing them with anyone beforehand. So I started building my ideas with my colleagues, who not only appreciated them, but they contributed to them. I found out that to be effective I had to build relationships with my colleagues. As I got into teaming, we all developed the ideas cooperatively."*

Here we see an example of conscious action, chosen from a solid foundation of awareness. This kind of action is an experiment and, because it is new, we don't know for sure what will happen. This means that active change involves risk. And here again are places where we can become stuck along the way.

For instance, we can criticize or ignore the answer. Let's say that we ask a question and we receive an answer. We may not like the answer we get, and we might argue with it. "That's a dumb answer!" Or the answer may provoke discomfort and we discount it. Whatever the reason, it is quite possible to become stuck with no change by ignoring the answers. Sometimes we may even stop asking questions when the answers are not convenient. Or we may keep asking questions until we get an answer that we find appealing and in this way prevent conscious change.

Another danger is to keep asking questions forever. We may feel we need to have all the information possible before we can take action. We ask question after question endlessly, in the hope that we will not miss a single scrap of data. The illusion here is that it is possible to know everything, including the outcome of an action, before acting. This goes beyond being well-informed. It's imagining that it is possible to eliminate all risk.

Another way we can become stuck is procrastination. This can include the methods described above as well as avoiding action in other ways. One common form of procrastination is to wait for someone else to act. Again, we hope to avoid risk, this time by letting someone else be the first to try out the experiment.

Yet another sticking place is to make no decision. Some of us become frozen in the stress of a situation and find it almost impossible to decide on an action. We might forget that not to make a decision is also a decision, but a reactive one. Applying the Active Change Model can help here.

Most of these blocks are about avoiding risk or having things the way we want, functional or not. Leaving things the same way, or clinging to particular outcomes, actually involves risk as well. We sometimes forget that we take risks by letting inaction or reactive action determine the outcome. Inevitably, all choices are risks. When we are unconscious, we can forget this fact.

> *Lou took a risk by asking what he might be contributing to his supervisor's behavior. "I realized that I had engaged in a power struggle with him. I felt indignant and thought he was a fool. I decided to let go of all that. What was the point, after all? I backed off and tried to participate in a flexible way. When he seemed defensive, I responded with calm reassurance, rather than by becoming defensive myself. I kept reminding myself that it's not about personal issues, but about all of us achieving the goals that we share." Lou had accepted his supervisor and was able to move on to his own new behavior. He was now acting differently.*

In the Act Step of the Active Change Model, we are talking about consciously choosing our action, which is different from reaction. Reaction is without questions, participation, or awareness of the meaning of our choices. The kind of active, aware action that we are discussing leads to healthy, functional change.

Change

> *Lou reported that eventually his entire work experience changed as a result of his personal change. "What started happening was that the ideas that we had all developed were presented jointly at meetings. Many of the ideas that I had originated were implemented with success. I was participating more without being stuck on having to come up with the answer all the time."*

Here we see the results of taking all of the steps described above. The change is an *active* change that occurs as a result of a consciously applied process. This is not change that has come from either reactivity or passivity. Change happens as a result of all of the actions involved in the active change model. It is the result we are seeking.

> *Lou was happier and more productive at his work than he had ever been. And all he did was change himself and his own behavior. And best of all, he told us, "Not only did my supervisor relax and open up more, but now he directly seeks me out to ask my opinions!" Lou changed to a healthier Lou who touched others. And Lou's change opened the way for others to change.*

The initial part of the change is when we *do* the new thing. We go to work in the grand laboratory of life and experiment. This in itself is a change. But the life of the process does not end here. When we do something new and different, we have a new event and a new result. Then we have something new to perceive, which brings us back to the beginning of our cycle. We describe, accept, question, and act, and this brings us again to a change.

Using the Active Change Model

The model is a description of what occurs when we are fully engaged in the change process. We can use this model to practice the skills necessary for conscious change. As we practice, we become more alert to the places that we can become stuck. In twenty years of using this model, we [the authors] have observed that the steps always happen in the order we have described. Again, in any substantial change there will be many cycles—millions, perhaps—that support and lead to the transformation.

In the following chapters, we will apply this model in various ways. The next chapter will focus on changing ourselves by first perceiving, describing, and accepting ourselves in a self-evaluation process, then developing a plan to apply the rest of the model. We feel that the best way to master change is from the inside out. This means that when we practice personal change in a conscious, active way, using this model, change is no longer a theory, but a personal experience. This is when we truly know something.

Personal Change Assessment

1. **Take a moment to recall a time when you successfully made a personal change. Remember as fully as you can the process that you used. Then jot down some answers to the following questions.**

   · Initially, what situation, event, or behavior did you notice?

   · How did you describe this to yourself or others?

   · In what ways did you accept it fully, somewhat, or only a little?

   · What questions did you ask of yourself and others?

   · How did the answers help you?

· What actions did you take?

· What were the results?

· Were there many cycles of change within this change?

2. **Consider for a moment: Is there a personal change that you are attempting at this time, but about which you feel stalled or stuck?**

   · What factors are you aware of so far?

   · How fully have you described them?

- Have you accepted the situation yet, or are you arguing with how "it, you, them" *should* be?

- What questions have you asked? What haven't you asked yet?

- Are the answers helpful?

- What actions have you tried so far?

- Considering the Active Change Model, what step are you in now?

2

Perceiving, Describing, and Accepting Who We Are

The Importance of Personal Change

A major theme of this book is that a change agent must actively practice personal change. Organization change essentially means that people within the organization change. If we, as change agents, live our life as changers, then we develop in ourselves the deepest experience of how people change and what they require in order to do it effectively. We cannot expect our clients to embrace change unless we embrace it ourselves.

As consultants, we are the instruments of change. The techniques we may use in our interventions is the music we play. Instruments vary enormously in their quality, tone, and range. We may play a fabulous piece of music, but the beauty of its sound will depend on the quality of the instrument it is played on. Because of this, the quality of our client work is the same as the quality of our selves personally. As change agents, we may have learned many techniques and theories and even practiced them. But until we practice change by changing our self, we will not truly be a leader for our clients' change. This is what mastering change from the inside out is all about.

To master change on the inside means to apply the Active Change Model vigorously to our own self. Of course, this begins with becoming conscious of who we really are. If we are unconscious of important aspects of our selves, we will impact our clients in unknown ways, and reactive change is likely. If we are aware of our capabilities and limitations, we can include that knowledge in our planning, all the while actively changing our self. In this way we can continue to grow in excellence, utilize our strengths, and compensate for our weaknesses.

The first steps of the Active Change Model are Perceive, Describe, and Accept. In this chapter we apply these steps to our selves in a personal way. In Chapter 3, we will apply them to our selves in relationship to the outcome of our client work.

About Personal Foundations

We, the authors, have identified ten core aspects of ourselves that we call our *Personal Foundations.* They are presented as a method that anyone can use to perceive and describe herself or himself more deeply. We developed these particular foundations after beginning with a larger number. They aren't intended to thoroughly describe every aspect of human beings, but to focus on the areas we thought were particularly applicable for practicing consultants. They are intended to serve as a useful model, not a definitive and comprehensive list. Individual practitioners who work with these foundations may well develop their own variations.

The Personal Foundations represent a number of basic aspects of human beings and, as such, they are universal. Every individual operates with each of these foundations. However, the *condition* of each foundation will be different for each person. The goal in focusing on them is to perceive and describe central aspects of who we are in a deep and instructive way.

While some of the Personal Foundations may also be considered values, we are not referring to them in that way. The foundations are a system for assessing our selves. They provide a way for us to study our selves and become more conscious of our own unique and current condition. For instance, a degree of integrity is present in everyone, but it will vary widely from one person to another. Careful examination of the *degree* of integrity present in oneself will help a person become more aware of who he or she is in this consequential area.

Learning more accurately and completely who we are as full and complex human beings is the beginning of conscious change. We humans do not necessarily change effectively simply by intending to become more developed individuals. In *An Invented Life,* Warren Bennis (1993) cites a Harris poll in which 90 percent of the people reported that they would dramatically change their lives if they could. To go further than desire and intent, we need to know *how* to change. And the beginning of the change process for all of us lies in looking deeply at ourselves and, in particular, at our Personal Foundations.

Taken together, the Personal Foundations form a kind of inner structure of our core selves. Depending on the state of each foundation, parts of the structure may be strong and cohesive, while other parts may not be very well-developed. If we visualize a geodesic sphere, with each strut of the sphere representing one of the foundations, we can have an image of how they all work together to form a struc-ture for our lives (see Figure 2.1). Strengthening any one of the foundations lends strength to the whole.

Figure 2.1. Geodesic Sphere

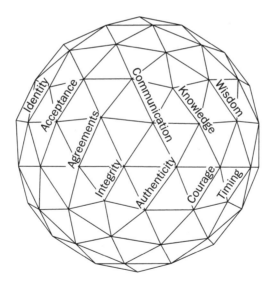

The foundations are presented and described below in detail, with exercises to help you assess yourself on each one. It is most important that you accept yourself just as you are as you work through this process. Later we will explore how you can strengthen the various Foundations in yourself by creating a Foundation Development Plan.

The Ten Personal Foundations

1. Identity
2. Acceptance
3. Agreements
4. Integrity
5. Authenticity
6. Courage
7. Timing
8. Knowledge
9. Communication
10. Wisdom

1. Identity

When we are clear about who we are and who we are not, we know our *identity*. With a strong sense of identity we can clearly and accurately know, name, and describe ourselves. A strong sense of identity is not shaken by the opinions of others. We can incorporate feedback from outside ourselves, but this feedback does not define who we are.

As we change, our identity changes. If we are consciously changing, we are continuously learning more about who we are, even as we simultaneously move into who we are becoming. Our awareness of our identity gives us a sense of continuity and connection to ourselves that helps us make choices based on our own unique characteristics.

> My greatest challenge in my youth was to figure out who I wanted to be. I was trained to be a "Southern Belle," which means I was raised to be an enabler. I wanted to be a competent Southern Belle, but at the same time I wanted to rule the world! I remember one of my early mentors saying to me, "I think

what confuses men about you is they are not sure if you are going to take care of them or kill them." I would be nice and sweet and Southern Belle-like until I could not control my assertiveness any more, and then the "real" me would come out.

Southern belles live in cocoons, trained not to notice or at least never to comment on anything unpleasant. So it was quite a shock to my family when, in the 1960s, I began to do civil rights work. I liked to think that I was not prejudiced. Then I would find myself encountering little pieces about my assumptions and stereotypes. Later, I began to work all around the globe. I've worked in over fifty countries with multiple cultural groups. I began to get it—that I don't know much of anything for sure!

Jane Magruder Watkins

We each have a sense of who we are—an identity—reflected in our personality and our physical, emotional, intellectual, and spiritual self. How accurate we are in our self-awareness of these aspects of ourselves will determine how well the choices we make will work for us.

Personality Identity

In the story above, Jane talks about the "Southern Belle" personality she was taught to have. As she became more conscious of her own personality, she let the old masks go. All of us have our own particular combinations of natural inclinations and style.

Almost everyone finds it intriguing to explore and describe personality. There are currently hundreds of methods of doing so, such as the popular Myers-Briggs Type Indicator. Our deep need to describe ourselves and others in terms of personality is probably as old as the human species. Beyond simple entertainment, it can be profoundly useful.

I have learned more about myself recently through my work with a strategic coach. I took a questionnaire, which essentially said, "I am at my best when I am present." For me this means that preparation and trying to have things figured out on the front end works to my disadvantage. I am at my best in my consulting work when I show up without over-preparing or planning.

Since then, I am present and attentive to what is going on around me. And it has been freeing for me to see it. At first it was risky. I worried: "Am I not doing my homework? Am I doing my job if I am not doing my homework?"

But the work is now easier; there is a flow-state with the people that I am working with and a permission for them to be more of who they are. And it is exceptional work.

One dimension of this is coming to terms with, accepting, and celebrating who I am. I am able to increase my own consciousness about how to do my best work and contribute and then tap into that whenever I can.

Robert "Jake" Jacobs

What we believe to be true about ourselves is a *foundation* from which we operate. The more accurate our belief is, the more connected we are with ourselves. Jake discovered that when he was over-prepared, he was less able to express himself authentically. He found out how to work within his own style, improved his work, and enjoyed himself even more than before. His relationship with himself and his activity is more solidly based on the truth of who he is, and the energy drain that comes from inaccuracy is gone.

We can use feedback from other people, introspection, personality tests, astrology, or anything that works to help us develop accurate self-descriptions of our personality. Are we friendly or reserved, quiet or talkative, generous or stingy? Ultimately, it is we who decide what we believe we are. Being accurate in this is like knowing what kind of vehicle we are driving: Is it a boat, train, plane, or car? If we know, we can get around a lot better.

Physical Identity

Like everything else in our human experience, our bodies are unique. Each of us has an endless amount of physical possibilities. As used here, physical identity is concerned not with visual appearance but the nature of the physical self. Some of us have more stamina than others, some are more active, some more athletic. Knowing the kind of body we have and then behaving accordingly is a key to balance, strength, and health.

I know that I am physically strong; my body heals quickly and is responsive. I also know that my body has limits, but I really haven't accepted those limits. I want my physical self to be like a one-ton, four-wheel-drive pickup truck. With a body like a truck, I could haul a big load anywhere. I could treat it roughly, and it would still go on and on, as long as I want. It would have so much power that even if it's poorly tuned, it still goes everywhere and anywhere. I behave as if this is true, and then crash myself in a wreck that takes a lot of time and work to recover from. My body really is more like a Porsche. It is finely tuned, flexible, and maneuverable. If I drive it like a truck, it will break. In this, I am a slow learner. Even though I "know" this about myself, I stubbornly hang on to what I want to be, not what I am. I am aware that I am stubborn and stuck in this. I am still learning to accept my physical self with its limits and gifts.

Renée M. Brown

Many of us ignore the messages that we receive about our physical selves. It is like taping over the gauges on our dashboards. We can begin to explore our identity in this area more deeply by asking, "Physically, what kind of person am I? Do I have any clues that my ideas about my physical self and the reality may be incongruent?"

Emotional Identity

There are two aspects of our emotional identity to look at. One is what we are like emotionally, and the other is what specific emotion we are feeling at a particular time.

Some of us may be quite emotional, but within our sense of identity we may believe that we are not emotional at all. We may have emotions, but not feel them. Our emotions will affect our behavior, but we will remain unconscious of how. When emotions are occurring in us but we remain disconnected from them, we are unable to separate what we feel from what we think.

On the other hand, if people are emotional and incorporate this into their identity, they can include this part of themselves in their choices. If they feel and recognize their emotions, rather than numbing them into the unconscious, their emotions can help signal them. If they know that an event is likely to upset them, they can prepare themselves by planning for a probable upset. When it happens, they can stay aware of what they are feeling without being surprised and losing their center. With this choice, they can stay more connected to what is happening in the moment, rather than getting overwhelmed or confused by the emotions.

More particularly, what emotion we feel at any given time is an important part of who we are. It is a clue to our individual identity. For example, ten people are in a meeting. Another person arrives late, apologizes, and tells a joke. While most of the ten might feel similarly about the event, none of them will feel exactly the same. The event is the same, but each individual responds differently on an emotional level. This response is a clue to what they are like as people.

Sometimes we may feel emotional, but we don't know which emotion it actually is. We might be angry and think we are sad, or feel as if something is wrong but tell ourselves it's really OK. Our emotions are a message, and if we hear them correctly, they can guide us. Naming our emotions accurately is a skill that we can develop. The beginning of this is done by perceiving, describing, and accepting the emotions that we *are* aware of. Then we can ask our selves questions to dig deeper and expand what we know. With this, our consciousness expands, and the Active Change Model is in full operation.

> When I was growing up, my family worked hard to contain emotions. There were seven children and things could get pretty wild. I remember some of my family sayings:
>
> "Big girls don't cry."
>
> "Go to your room until you straighten out."
>
> "Keep a stiff upper lip."
>
> "Don't you dare get angry with me, little girl."
>
> I grew up with a smile on my face because that was an acceptable expression of emotion in the house. No matter what was going on, I was smiling.
>
> Later, as an adult, I remember getting feedback on a work performance review that "others were concerned" because I was always smiling, "even in difficult situations." That was one of the first times I became aware of what I was doing. I had never learned to name my emotions correctly and did not have a clue about how to express emotions in a healthy way.
>
> I took a class from Renée on "emoting." It was designed to help participants touch, name, and release our emotions in a healthy way. I was terrified of what would come up. I was afraid that I would release so much anger or sadness that I would not recover! In the two weeks between classes, we had homework. Each person paired up with another student and practiced our assignment. One of us facilitated the other for an hour, and then we switched. Each time, we practiced a new technique to help us open up to buried emotions.
>
> One technique we practiced was the contradiction exercise, which was to say statements that were a contradiction to the emotional block. For example, repeatedly saying, "I love my body," "I am happy all the time," or "I feel safe in new situations." This would help to uncover the buried emotions.

I got really good at facilitating first and extending the session so that my turn to feel was shortened. By the end of the year, I realized it wasn't so bad after all and signed up for this class two more times!

Kristine Quade

When we are more conscious of our own emotions, we will not easily be carried away by what everyone else is feeling. We stay more centered in our own opinions and viewpoints. If someone tells us what he or she thinks we should feel, we might respond, "That might be your opinion, but it is not what I *am feeling.*" Most of us can think of a time when a whole group was swayed in a direction they did not want to go, simply because as individuals they were not aware of how they really felt or because they became convinced that how they were feeling was wrong.

Intellectual Identity

The intellectual realm, usually thought of in terms of intelligence or education, actually encompasses the whole mind as both a container of facts and a user of knowledge. In terms of our intellectual identity, it is important to understand what we don't know as well as what we do know. Also, are we actually using the information we have? And can we be both certain and flexible at the same time?

Most of our intellectual identity probably comes from comments by family, teachers, and other adults. We have listened to and believed what we have heard. If we believe we are not smart, and actually are, then we cannot fully use our potential. If we think we are smarter than we are, we have a gap between our self-image and our true capabilities.

> *Growing up, "Thomas" was exceptionally creative, but his teachers and parents often criticized him for not doing his homework, not paying attention in class, and distracting other students. This followed him into college, where he kept dropping out of classes. He finally found a school where he could take one class a month, which fit his attention style. In his work life, Thomas worked a lot of hours and had many creative ideas, but performance reviews indicated he was not performing to the standards of the rest of the group due to his lack of organization and follow-through. This affected Thomas's self-esteem, confidence, and ambition.*
>
> *A friend gave him a book about Adult Attention Deficit Disorder, which said that common ADD symptoms were distractibility, over or under focus, disorganization, and forgetfulness. Thomas learned that children with ADD are often hyperactive, which he was.*

*Most people with ADD feel they are not as smart or capable as others. Some
even feel they are lazy, crazy, or dumb. Many people with ADD are relieved to discover that there is a reason that they can't do things the same way that others can.*

*Thomas learned all he could about ADD and, with the help of his counselor,
learned some strategies to cope with issues around time and project management.
He purchased a computer program to help with project management so schedul-
ing could be fun. He also purchased an electronic calendar to have with him at
all times. Thomas also learned how helpful it was to talk about this with his co-
workers. He discovered others with ADD, and they acted as a support group for
him. He began to feel a lot better about himself. He was more productive and successful at taking his creative ideas and making them a reality.*

In Thomas's case, people told him he was not intellectual and he believed them.
He later found that not to be true. Thomas found out about an important part of
himself, which was that he had ADD. This helped him to understand how his own
mind worked. It is important that we develop our own sense of who we are and
our true uniqueness

Spiritual Identity

Our spiritual identities involve our beliefs about the meaning of life and our place
within it. Everyone has a philosophy, belief system, or religion that defines for him
or her what life is about. Some have found beliefs that help them have healthy and
fulfilling lives. Others have beliefs that create cynicism and disconnection. When
we are conscious of our own personal sense of life's meaning and purpose, we can
examine how well these beliefs are working for us. A strong spiritual identity
means that we are clear about what we believe and about how those beliefs can
support us in being healthy and whole human beings.

I believe that I have given myself a grandiose assignment: To change the world
into a loving, peaceful, and welcoming place where people accept others for
who they are and, at the same time, to have the courage to speak out when I
see something that I feel is evil. I was called to do this work—it is not a job.
It gives me a sense of self-worth, of being valued, even admired by others,
friendship, and reciprocal work. I am happiest and most centered when my
work is both giving and receiving.

In recent years, the most valuable contribution to my work has been my
growing understanding of and comfort with a social constructionist view of

human systems, which is why I like Appreciative Inquiry so much. I know that no one's social constructed view is more valuable than another person's. In fact, what is real for people in a village in Kenya is real for them regardless of how I see and understand their world. I learned that if I wanted to relate to people, I have to try to understand the world as they see it.

Jane Magruder Watkins

Exercise

This exercise is designed to help you think about and verbalize your identity.

Write a letter to yourself. In it, describe yourself in the third person. The letter can begin as follows: "Dear (Me), I want you to know all you can about (me with an alias). Here is what I can tell you about her/him so far. . . ."

---

2. Acceptance

Acceptance is to fully acknowledge our state of being. In order to practice conscious, active change, we must experience acceptance as part of the process. If we are judgmental, condemning, or critical, acceptance will not be a strong foundation for us. Acceptance makes it possible to begin to change things that we might disagree with. By accepting ourselves as we are, we are free to improve, rather than staying caught up in whether what we did was wrong or right or whether we were "bad." In practicing self-acceptance, we can have remorse about past events that we regret, but we can let go of condemning ourselves about them.

I stress self-acceptance in my work because I have found it to be a crucial factor in my own life. It is the gateway to my personal and professional effectiveness.

Over the years I have tended to play down my accomplishments and make more of my mistakes instead of giving myself credit for what I have done. I err on the side of self-deprecation. It has been easier for me to accept others than to accept myself. This is harmful because it is not based on a balanced view of reality. I have tried to work on this because it limits my effectiveness.

When I accept myself without conditions, I have more self-confidence and freedom of thought and action. Self-acceptance becomes a way to empower myself to use my talents and abilities. When I accept myself conditionally, I limit myself and fail to model effective actions. I become self-conscious instead of other-conscious. Encouraging others to move beyond self-limiting beliefs requires modeling the behavior as well as suggesting it to them. I can't suggest what I don't model without being hypocritical.

When I find myself being self-deprecating, I make a point to stop doing it. For example, instead of celebrating a success, in the past I would simply move on to the next thing. I didn't want to be perceived as arrogant, but self-deprecation is just as destructive. Now I try to stop, acknowledge that I have persevered, believed in myself, and done what I could do to accomplish something and that what I did is good enough. And then I celebrate the moment. That translates into a higher quality of self-acceptance.

Ken Hultman

When we accept ourselves, our relationship with the past shifts—we can let go of what is already over and move on. How easy is it to change when someone else is glaring down at you with criticism and judgment? It's the same when we judge ourselves—we get stuck and cannot change.

Children learning to walk demonstrate the absence of self-judgment beautifully. At this age children have not yet learned to feel "wrong" for making a mistake. They toddle around, falling down and getting up over and over. Imagine if every time they fell down they said to themselves, "Oh, I'm such a klutz! When will I ever learn? I must be bad." Their willingness to try again would disappear.

We are also prevented from changing when we get stuck on the other end of the spectrum. Here we hold onto inflated ideas of how we are "good" or "better than," fiercely protecting these ideas from any feedback to the contrary. When we do this, we have more invested in staying the same than in changing.

It is important to note that being accepting is not about being unemotional or detached. We can accept our behavior and still have feelings about it. We may approve of our behavior and want to do more of it, or we may disapprove and want to do less. We can be *discerning* without being *judgmental*. When we *discern*, we perceive and describe in acceptance. To *discern* is to accurately describe the status of a given individual, group, or situation. To *judge* is to consider an individual, group, or situation right or wrong for being as it is. Describing accurately is essential to any successful change. Judging always obstructs.

Exercise

How accepting of yourself are you? Use the following exercise to begin to explore your level of self-acceptance.

Listen carefully to the speeches you make to yourself.

- Do you ruminate about how you "could" or "should" have done better?

- Do you tell yourself about how well you did, while dismissing criticism?

- How would you feel if someone else said the same things to you as you say to yourself?

- Do you tell yourself the same things your parents said?

---

3. Agreements

Our society runs on agreements. Whether we are conscious or unconscious of them, we have agreements that provide a framework in which we live. Our social behavior and manners are agreements that we take for granted. We agree that a particular behavior is desirable or good, while other behaviors are offensive. Social protocol, business protocol, and diplomatic protocol are not laws of nature—they are agreements. The nature of these agreements will have a large impact on how we function. For example, when we have jobs, we agree to show up at a certain time and perform in a certain way, while our employer also makes agreements. In different cultures, what it means to have a job may be governed by different sets of agreements.

Many of the agreements that govern our lives were made before we were born. No one asked for our opinion or approval, and we usually agree to go along. Our society depends on agreements that everyone more or less agrees to, and the force of these cultural agreements is powerful. However, there are many agreements in which we have more opportunity for individual formation and creativity.

When we decide what we want to do, who we want to be, or what values we want to govern our lives, we have formed an agreement with ourselves. Our behavior follows the agreements we have made. Until we change our agreements with ourselves, our behavior will not change. However, if we perceive and describe what our current self-agreements are and accept them, we are on the way to conscious active change. We can create the agreements that we want to live by consciously.

I was in Mississippi when Martin Luther King was killed. He was such an icon for me. I remember watching the TV and thinking, "I will never again hear a racist remark without confronting it." I envisioned myself as a warrior confronting all racist remarks. This gave me the courage to be able to say to others, "That makes me uncomfortable" or "You might look at that a different way." I try not to judge others for seeing it the way they do. But I try to be clear about my own beliefs and values. This has had a huge impact on where and how I work.

Fifteen or twenty years ago, I worked in a system in which there was a lot of talk about equality, equity, and collaboration. It didn't take me long to realize that the behavior within the organization did not match the rhetoric. I experienced a lot of covert racism in the system, as well as a lot of subtle ways to punish people who did not conform to the system's version of reality. Even worse, the collusion was so pervasive that it was nearly impossible to have a healthy difference of opinion about values and realities. I could not confront things like racism or hierarchy because it was not out in the open. It took me a long time to realize I could not work there.

When I became clear about this, I left because I could not be consistent with my agreement with myself to live my own values, particularly those about confronting racism. Years later I was invited back to work with the organization. I decided not to because I was afraid that I would find the same situation.

Jane Magruder Watkins

Jane affirmed an agreement she had made with herself about the kind of organization and work she would participate in. This kind of agreement forms a boundary. In this example, her boundary is about what kind of work she agrees to do and what kind of system she is able to work in.

Boundaries are what delineate the difference between who I am and my domain and who you are and your domain. For instance, who decides who we are? If I have made an agreement with myself that I am the one who decides who I am, rather than agreed that it is others who define me, the difference in the outcome will be enormous. If someone comes along and tells me that I am this or that kind of person, I can decide whether I agree with that opinion or not. This indicates a boundary I have set about who ultimately determines my sense of self. If I accept another's opinion as a factual description of me without my own input or evaluation, I have not established a boundary. In this situation, my identity will change with everyone else's opinion, and my sense of self will weaken.

The following questions can help us discover and strengthen our boundaries:

- Have I agreed to make this my responsibility either explicitly or implicitly?
- Who are my agreements with?
- Who, if anyone, has been asked to do or say something here?
- Are the agreements that are in place being respected?
- Is anyone assuming responsibility rather than discussing and re-negotiating?

> When I facilitate an event planning team, I start with a clear sense of me and a fuzzy sense of them. By the time we have done the work of telling our stories and consensing on the purpose, I know them; I have them in my body. But I know the difference; I still know me as well. With that knowledge, I will argue something that I know is for them, not me. The best piece of advice I can give on knowing boundaries is to get help until you know. It is the most important thing for a consultant to do, to know where I end and you begin. Then I won't encroach on your space.
>
> *Kathy Dannemiller*

With clear boundaries, we are aware that every choice we make is really ours to make. We do not give our free will away to others, nor do we attempt to take another's free will from them. We are willing to stick with the agreements we make or else negotiate changes. We do not arbitrarily act on what is convenient for us, thereby forcing others to adjust to us. And we don't arbitrarily adjust to others if it means compromising ourselves or other agreements we have made.

Ultimately, every choice we make is an agreement. It is always an agreement with our self: "Yes, I will do this now" or "No, I won't do this." Our choice may also be an agreement with others: "OK, I want to buy this" or "No, not now." Even if we feel "forced" into doing something, we really are not. The reality is that we may *decide* that the consequences of not agreeing to do something may best be avoided, so we *decide* to agree. This means that we *choose* what to agree with based on the best available opportunity.

Exercise

To begin exploring your agreements and boundaries, complete the following exercise.

First, go through the following questions from the frame of your relationship with yourself and your life. Then, go through them again from the frame of your relationship with another person (mate, friend, client, and so on).

- How do the agreements I have in place help me/others expand our lives?

- In what ways do these agreements set clear boundaries or not?

- If I change my agreements what do I think will happen?

- Am I willing to take the risk?

---

4. Integrity

Integrity is an allegiance to life-giving behaviors. This means that we are committed to behave in a way that nurtures more life for all. Low integrity is an allegiance to selfish needs without regard for how others are affected.

Integrity involves the personal rules that we live by. A high level of integrity includes a strong value system of caring for our selves as well as for others. A person with high integrity does not compromise this value for the sake of comfort or convenience. When we have high integrity, we understand the impact of our behavior and choices. We choose life and self-respect as our priority over considerations of pain or reward.

Often, when we talk about integrity, we are concerned with how it affects other people. Here we are talking about integrity as it affects our relationship with our life and ourselves.

Many years ago I went shopping for towels at a department store. They were on sale, so I bought three full sets. At least I thought I bought them. When I got in my car and looked at the receipt, I discovered that the clerk had only charged me for two sets. So I took the towels and receipt back into the store, found the clerk, and asked him to correct his mistake. I think it is sad that the clerk was surprised.

> When I originally went into the store, our agreement was that I would buy and they would sell, not that I would steal, no matter how easy they made it for me. Even if no one else would know that I stole the towels, I would know. This is not who I am, or who I want to be. Ultimately, I live with myself, and respecting myself is worth far more than any price.
>
> *Renée M. Brown*

If we want others to honor and value us, we need to live in a way so that we also honor and value ourselves. Asking ourselves whether we would be proud to have our actions described in the newspaper can help to tell us whether those actions have integrity. With weak integrity, we believe that making life easy and comfortable for ourselves is our primary goal, regardless of the cost to others or to ourselves. With strong integrity, we believe that there is a way to achieve excellence without harming ourselves or anyone else. With a high level of personal integrity, we carry our ethics and values everywhere we go, and the bottom line is that our integrity is not negotiable.

Exercise

In this chapter, we are examining how the current condition of our integrity affects our own self and our life. The following questions are designed to help you do that:

- Remember a time when you were pleased with yourself and your actions. How did your integrity play a role in this?
- Remember a time when you felt diminished or less than you usually feel. What happened that relates to your integrity?
- What actions have you taken that have resulted in you feeling more alive and whole?

---

5. Authenticity

Authenticity means that we present to the world and ourselves the truth of who and what we are. When we are authentic, we have stopped waiting for someone else to give us permission to be our true selves. It means we can function on the basis of what actually is, rather than on what we pretend is.

Authenticity has no guarantee of safety; it is a guarantee of aliveness. Everyone seems to agree that authenticity is a good thing, so why don't we practice it more? Authenticity feels risky. What if people didn't like us? Or approve of us? What if they attacked us? And they might—it's a very real risk. When we are focused on the risks of being authentic, we usually fail to consider the risks of keeping our masks and shields in place. The cost of these is a loss of our life force and of our self.

What our masks cost depends on our values. We use our masks to manipulate. With a mask, we take on a role. This role is usually calculated to maximize personal safety and power. For example, when we pretend we know more than we really do, we feel safer because we are seen as smarter, with more authority. Most of us do this occasionally; some do this all the time.

When we act out this inauthentic role, what are we really saying to ourselves? One message is that the "real" me is so awful that people will attack me if they see me as I truly am. Another message is that I am not good enough as I am. And I am also saying something about the people in my life, such as, "They will hurt me if they know the real me. They are hurtful people, and I am too weak to ever recover from what they might do to me." Or possibly I am saying about them, "They won't give me authority if they know the real me. They have to be manipulated into respect." Are these really the messages we want to give our selves and others?

Usually we create our masks and shields quite unconsciously. And then they operate beneath the surface of our awareness, until we pry open the lid with questions. As we become conscious of them, we can use the Active Change Model to make conscious choices about how we present ourselves to ourselves and to the rest of the world.

> Authenticity is when my behavior, thoughts, and feelings fit with the person that I know I am and am becoming. Am I congruent in my identity? Authenticity means that I can identify myself in various settings and media (in a book, single person, small group, six hundred people, audiotape, online) and that people experience the same person each time. I will not see me and they will not see me as someone who is different because of the situation. I won't have a series of identities.
>
> *Geoff Bellman*

When we are connected to both ourselves and to others, we experience self-congruence as well as congruence between ourselves and others. When we examine our degree of authenticity, we will probably find that, whenever we are not authentic, we are betraying ourselves.

> Authenticity is being true to who I am and being true to you about who I am.
> What you see is what you get. I may not be lovable but it is who I am.
>
> *Kathy Dannemiller*

Exercise

To begin evaluating your own level of authenticity, consider the following questions:

- How do you know when you are being authentic with yourself?
- What masks and shields do you maintain with others?
- How does it affect you to hold these in place?
- What would happen if you removed them?

---

6. Courage

In this time of accelerated change, we are all confronted with the need to do things differently and, in fact, to become different. Both our inner and outer worlds are challenged to meet this need with flexibility and creativity. Change brings with it risk, obstacles, resistance, and discomfort, and living with today's demands for excellence and achievement requires enormous courage.

Courage is not an inherent quality—it is developed. As with physical exercise, when we stretch our courage, it becomes stronger. Every day we encounter opportunities to do this. For instance, it takes enormous courage to choose truth over personal safety. Every time we speak our truth, our courage becomes stronger. If we routinely perform conscious acts of healthy behavior in spite of our fear, we will develop formidable courage.

> By the time I was 40, I had a full tenured position in a prestigious academic situation, with a foundation chair and all the perks. All of these external benefits were proof that I was my father's good daughter. I was an inside consultant and could have stayed on that path.

One winter, I had a series of dreams that told me I needed to save my life fast by getting out. The dreams were not literal; they were not about my job. They were about my psyche—about the need to get out of my position as my father's daughter in such a way that I would not join with the angry voices of that generation of U.S.-centric feminism, which were pointing fingers at all men, that I would deal with my misogyny. I was not living in an environment where I could learn more about the practice of my female authority. If I did not change my path, I would remain a father's daughter all my life and replicate the leadership model I wanted to destroy.

The dreams were so strong, and the last one shook me so hard, that the next day I resigned without a business plan and gave up all the perks. There was no net underneath the trapeze, yet it felt like an act to save my life. I did not know how I was going to do it.

Alexandra Merrill

We all have the opportunity to live a script that someone else has written. It seems we need a great deal of courage to live our *own* scripts.

Many of us find success almost as scary as failure. Because of this, we may have placed self-imposed limits on our freedom to fully engage our selves in our lives. When a project has failed, are we willing to see how we may have contributed to its failure or what we can learn? And do we have the courage to own up to our own successes? If we are holding ourselves back, we can change that, but again, it takes courage.

Courage follows commitment. If we are committed to quality work, personal excellence, and healthy functioning, this becomes the focus of our efforts. Our commitment will call forth our courage. In the same way, enthusiasm bolsters courage. We often repress our enthusiasm instead of cultivating it. Let's bring it out, flesh it out, pump it up! It is like a fresh wind in our sails. When we keep it going, it feeds our courage.

Exercise

How courageous are you? Begin to assess your level of courage by reflecting on one or more of the following questions:

- Describe the last thing you did that required courage.

- What were some of the turning points in your life that required courage?

- What is something that you regularly do that requires courage?

- How is your life different today because of challenges you have met with courage?

7. Timing

Timing is about development and readiness. It is about understanding that change happens within a time process and about respecting the limits imposed by time, while also being awake to opportunities as they arise.

> For me, timing is about stepping into the river and going with the flow of the system. It is not about coming in with prescriptions but rather hanging loose and being flexible. Timing is being able to understand what is needed in the moment.
>
> *Jane Magruder Watkins*

Sometimes people do not allow themselves to have stages of development. They tell themselves that they should be better or further along than they are—that they should already be complete or finished. They may have received this message from their families, and they now continue it on their own. Our culture reinforces the expectation of having everything *now.*

The fact is, we live and develop in time. We don't expect newborn babies to walk and talk. We don't even try to teach them how. They tell us when they are ready by attempting to walk and by making jabbering sounds. They learn the skills when they are ready and able, not before.

However, many of us were pushed as we were growing up. We may have been told that we really should be behaving better, even if we were not yet capable of that behavior—when we are three, we should behave as a five-year-old or when we are sixteen, we should behave as an adult. Then, as soon as our behavior improves, the bar is raised. In some families, it's the opposite. Children may be over-protected and told that they are not yet old enough to handle new things.

This sort of experience can prevent us from learning a sense of timing for ourselves. We learn to push forward or hold back, depending on our response to the pressures. This becomes our habitual relationship to time, and we lose touch with our own knowing of readiness. We can practice discovering our own timing with our use of the Active Change Model.

We begin with our consciousness that we have timing and that we may not be aware of it. Then, we agree with our selves to include the question of timing as we contemplate our choices. Then, as we live the result of our choices, we continue to observe these results, including the factor of timing. We learn from our real-time experiences and observations. As we continue to do this, our knowledge of our timing is strengthened.

Each step of our journey of change can be viewed as containing treasure. These treasures hold valuable information that helps with learning, growing, and changing and that prepares us for the next step. If we reach a step without having gained the treasure from the step before, we will be unable to understand the next experience or to move through it effectively. This is *timing*.

> Making myself retire has not been easy to do. I asked myself:
>
> Who am I if I am not working?
>
> How do I learn if I am not in the world connecting with people?
>
> What does it mean to be at home and at rest?
>
> I struggled with this because of my health. I did not know how to set down my work. Retirement was like sitting in the bathroom and not talking to anyone. So I decided to go to a place where no one could reach me for a month to gather data in isolation about what retirement feels like. The first year did not work because I couldn't keep myself in isolation. The second year I went for two months!
>
> Before I left on the second trip, I talked to a friend who said, "You have this passion to know where you are going and to have a sense of the goal so you can make the choices to get there. You love thinking five years ahead. What you *really* love is thinking ten years ahead. If you are truly to triumph in retirement, you need to set this down. While you are in England and Scotland with no phone, don't ask the question, 'Who am I going to be in five or ten years?' You can't ask the question, *because the answer is not ready for you.* You have always struggled, looking inside to determine where you want to be. Can you live for two months without asking the question?"
>
> I experienced every stage of death and dying and it was the most depressing time of my life. It was all inside of me. My friends did not see it. But on the inside, the Action Research wheel was trying to figure out what it all meant. In the fall, I had the answer and went to see Peggy Lippitt [wife of Ron

Lippitt]. I told her, "I have the answer! It is not what I want to *do* but *who I want to be.* I had the wrong question all along: Retirement is about BEING." Peggy said, "I knew you would get there eventually!"

Kathy Dannemiller

Timing can be a difficult concept to grasp. To help make it more concrete, we suggest the following exercise.

Exercise

Achieving a goal is a change process. Pick a goal that you have and consider your progress toward that goal. Answer the following questions:

- What have you accomplished so far?
- Where are you (beginning, middle, end) on the road toward achievement of the goal?
- Do you know what your next step is?
- Do you tend to hold yourself back too long? Are you doing that now?
- Do you tend to push yourself too hard? Are you doing that now?
- Is this a time when you need to push? To rest? To wait? To reestablish your foundations?

---

8. Knowledge

Knowledge is a form of awareness. Awareness brings choice, choice brings movement, and movement brings freedom. Every piece of information we have is a tool, and the more we know, the more tools we have. The most important kinds of information are those that help us know how to do something.

When I was in high school, Dad gave me a little two-person sailboat. Our family had always had powerboats and water skis—I had never even ridden on a sailboat before. We lived on a small bay in California, so I carried the little boat down to the dock, put it in, and sailed away. I let the sail out and went wherever the wind pushed me. I ended up in a little corner by the sea wall, and the harbor patrol came along and towed me home. This was great fun, so

I went out sailing frequently, always with the same result. I wondered how it was that the other sailboats didn't end up in the same cul-de-sac with me. I often took friends out with me, and one day the friend I was with actually knew how to sail! She taught me how to tack with the wind, zigging and zagging all over the place. The miracle was that now I was free to sail anywhere I wanted! And I did.

Since then, I've come to view sailing as a metaphor for navigating through life. Sailing works on the laws of the physics of the wind, the boat, the rudder and the sail. Life has its own set of metaphysics. Every choice we make has a result, just like in sailing. I decided that since I spend more time living than sailing, I would be wise to study life and the way it works.

Renée M. Brown

In terms of knowledge as a Personal Foundation, we are not necessarily focusing on knowing lots of "facts." While formal education is certainly a part of our knowledge, we have the opportunity to learn throughout our lifetime. This becomes a way of life.

We shortchange ourselves in the knowledge department if we imagine we have learned all there is to know about anything. This is when our questions die and we stay the same, while the world continues to expand. An open, inquiring mind is our asset here. We can also know that we don't have to know everything. If we think we do, it may be difficult to focus on doing what we really want to do.

One of the things that I feel as I grow older is that there is more freedom not to have to be good at everything and that I can be more open and honest with clients about how I feel. For example, if someone asks me to do work design, I might say, "I love working with you guys, but I have not done work design, so let's talk about this and explore other options, which might include partners or alliances." I find that I am not scurrying around looking for people to coach me on how to do what I don't know how to do. I am being honest and telling the client when I don't know how to do what they are asking me to do. When I was younger, I needed to build experience and was not this honest.

Barbara Bunker

While it may not be important that we know *everything*, it seems that the most successful consultants have a deep passion for learning.

I received a Master Coach certification in 1997. I was struggling with the concept of mastery as it applied to me. I was uncomfortable with the extra respect that I received from other coaches. I am just Jim Earley, just a guy. Then I read George Leonard's book on mastery, where I learned that mastery is really the outcome of being a lifelong student. I realized I was not honoring the respect of other coaches by my not taking mastery seriously. I realized that the bottom line is that I love to learn everything. I can learn and be comfortable with that. I can then be considered a master.

Jim Earley

Exercise

To begin thinking about your level of knowledge, answer the following questions:

- How would you describe your knowledge generally?

- What is your attitude toward learning?

- What do you do when you don't know how to do something?

- What are you currently doing in your life to extend your knowledge?

---

9. Communication

Effective communication has several aspects: listening with the heart, the mind, and the ears, as well as speaking with our whole selves. Communication is expression. When we express ourselves to others in any way, we are sharing a part of ourselves. When we receive the expressions of others, we are allowing them to touch us with who they are as well as with what they are saying.

We express ourselves not only with words but with body language, emotions, tone of voice, actions, art, and music and in innumerable other ways. The more completely we share ourselves in our communication, the clearer we are. The more completely we listen, using our whole selves, the more the messenger as well as the message will touch us.

It is possible to have an instant insight that literally dissolves the pathways and makes the ruts disappear. That happens when you touch someone's heart; it does not happen when you touch someone's head. So, in coaching, I need to find the stories, metaphors, et cetera, that touch the heart where there is a choice to do something different from what they have been doing before. I need to say it in such a way that the individual gets it.

I look for language flexibility and stories that touch the heart. It is like I am a halfback. A fullback forces the way open—a halfback looks for a hole in the line. I am looking for the language that gets me inside. Forcing myself inside is touching their head, not their heart. They have to allow me in. If I can help them feel they are their own, they have let me inside.

Jim Earley

Communication is not just about relating with others. We also communicate with ourselves. We talk to ourselves with thoughts, emotions, actions, and in many other ways. And we listen to ourselves as well. We have a constant internal dialogue. Are our communication skills with ourselves as effective as with others?

In an ideal world, we could all be open to listen and hear wholeheartedly, with others and with ourselves. However, most of us have various blocks and hang-ups in this area. These keep us from fully experiencing and sharing with others. If we cannot share what we have to say, we are not free. And if we cannot hear what others are saying, we are alone.

I have always talked too much. I am a big extrovert. As I talk, I learn. I am passionate about learning, and I always want to learn what I am thinking. Some years ago I had a profound experience that has helped me to work on really being present and listening to the other.

I spent an hour with the Dalai Lama. A small group of us were talking about a project with his government. We did most of the talking, but when we left, each of us felt that he had talked to us individually. . . . He was so totally present, I felt heard and respected. I would like to be that kind of presence.

Jane Magruder Watkins

Listening with the Heart, Mind, and Ears

We call listening with the heart, mind, and ears *authentic listening*. This is because it means listening from a state of truly wanting to know. This includes paying attention to someone else or our own self by listening in a state of discovery, acceptance, compassion, and mutual seeking. This means we get our own agendas, ideas, and projections out of the way.

To listen with our *hearts* is to listen with compassion, and it involves seeking full understanding without judgment. This is when we care about who we are listening to, regardless of whether we agree or disagree, or even of whether we like or dislike the person. We know that we will never really know what it is to be another, but we still seek to witness the person's world as fully as possible. When we listen with our hearts, we do so without insisting that the other person listen to us in the same way, or even at all.

To listen with our *minds* is to seek knowledge, and it is an opportunity to learn what other people know and think. Do we know what they've been saying clearly enough to be able to explain it to someone else? How often do people assume they know what someone else is talking about? If we assume that we do not understand what we have heard and ask a few questions to check it out, we might be surprised at the gaps in our hearing.

To listen with our *ears* is to pay careful attention both to the literal words that are being used as well as to the tone and inflection of the voice. Our brain is designed to fill in the blanks, and it tends to fill them in with familiar ideas or images. We often do not hear what is actually being said but rather our interpretation, both in terms of the actual words and of their tone. To combat this tendency, we can assume that we are interpreting and then practice giving feedback and performing other reality checks.

We are not actually listening if we are worrying primarily about ourselves and about how we might be perceived. People with weak listening skills are busy thinking that they already know what the other person is saying or what they are going to say when it is their turn to speak—thinking about anything, in fact, except what is actually happening in the present moment.

One reason that confident people function so well is because they are able to pay attention to others without fussing over themselves. When we are actually listening, we are connected with the fact that people are interested in being heard and understood, and we are not preoccupied with what they think about us.

Asking Questions

Chapter 4 is devoted to the nature of questions and includes exercises to build expertise for developing our skills in this area. In this section, we will make some preliminary points about the practice of questioning.

Every question carries assumptions and implications. Very often we imagine that we know far more than we actually do. Because we so often mistake our assumptions for facts, we neglect to ask questions that would be beneficial. When we develop an attitude of healthy curiosity, wanting to know the truth, our questions become productive and revealing. Questions are the most powerful tool we have for discovery.

Questions open doors for communication. How often do we not really understand someone or something, but fail to ask any questions? With questions we can connect deeply with another person. When we ask questions, we are participating, not just passively sitting on the sidelines. Although it is true that we risk something with every question we ask, it is also true that we risk something with every question we do not ask.

Speaking Clearly

Speaking is not only about saying what others need to hear, but also about speaking up for ourselves. We can say something just to "get it off our chests." It is healing to be heard by others. Sometimes simply making a statement for our selves is particularly empowering. Even though most people claim not to believe in reading minds, it seems that most of us expect others to do so. Here again we confront a dangerous assumption: Imagining that others know what we are thinking.

It seems obvious that we need to speak understandably, yet not everyone does. This skill comes easily for some, but is extremely difficult for others. There are many causes of incoherent speaking, and we need to understand them:

- We might unconsciously be afraid of being heard.
- We might have developed a "blind spot" where we miss connections between what we are thinking and what we are saying.
- We might be imagining that the listeners do not really want to hear us.
- We might want to just get the situation over with because we are terrified of speaking.
- We may not notice clues that let us know whether the listeners are following along.
- We may be disconnected from our audience.
- We might need more experience and practice.
- We might be nervous about being held accountable for what we say.

Exercise

Following are some suggestions for ways to practice and evaluate your communication skills.

- Tape record a meeting at which you are speaking. Afterward, listen as objectively as possible for a sense of your clarity. How do others in the meeting respond to you?

- Ask a coach to listen to you speak and to give you candid feedback and help.

- Repeat to others what you think they said to see whether you heard it accurately.

- Take some voice lessons. We often do not speak understandably because of unconscious restriction in the use of our voice. Not only does voice training open up the tone and sound of the voice, but a by-product seems to be a clearer connection between the brain and the voice.

---

10. Wisdom

Wisdom is knowledge applied in present time. When we have wisdom, it means that in each moment of choice we are in contact with all of our experience and knowledge. We all have experience and knowledge; the difference between the wise and unwise is that the wise weave together all that they know. Wisdom is the ability to use our knowledge in new ways. We create a synthesis of all that we know for each unique choice.

> Wisdom: When wise, we are flexible. I like this best. Being able to ride the roller coaster and enjoy it—every moment is a new now.
>
> *Jane Magruder Watkins*

Unlike wisdom, knowledge is something we learn. Knowledge is data—it is not flexible. We acquire knowledge from study, observation, and personal experience. Then we use what we know—this is the beginning of becoming wise. Wisdom is a quality that we can cultivate. We do this by using everything we know in a flexible way in every situation. We develop a quality of thinking in which we apply what we have learned to new situations. When we think in compartments, all that we know is not easily available to us to use.

All of us have certain patterns of behavior that we repeat over and over. We may even know that they lead to problems rather than solutions, but we may still do them. It seems we are convinced that someday the pattern will work, but it rarely does. This is where the expression "Wise up!" comes from—the need to see our lives realistically, then make appropriate choices. This includes understanding what we can and cannot do.

All of us fall into an emotional pit now and then. Some of us fall more often than others; some fall deeper than others. We think that life is just too much, and we feel hopeless. Sometimes we believe that the pit is all there is, and we refuse to take any action. While it is not unwise to find ourselves in difficulty, it is unwise to believe that that is all there is, overwhelming anything we might do. The exercise of wisdom brings forth our knowledge of life in its fuller context: No downfall is permanent; there is always help, there is always hope, there is always something to learn. If we remember what we have done earlier in our lives, we can get out the tools that we used to dig ourselves out the last time—or we can have the wisdom to ask for help and guidance.

Wisdom is a foundation that really incorporates all of the other ones. When we exercise wisdom:

- We know what we know and what we do not know.
- We know who we are and who we are not.
- We know our strengths and weaknesses.
- We know our goals and priorities.
- We know how to find help.
- We know how to give help.

I think wisdom is "being" wise, not "doing" wise. I was wise when I was younger. What made it easier for me was growing up in the world's most affirming family. I never had any question about being special. There are others who are wise but have had to work harder because they had difficult lives when growing up. What I like about being conscious and continually doing

Action Research with both life and career is that I am learning—always on a learning journey that can only result in BEING wise.

Kathy Dannemiller

A final definition of wisdom: When we make wise choices, the outcome is the best possible for everyone concerned. We only know that for sure after the fact.

Exercise

Take a moment to write out your definition of wisdom.

·   How are you practicing it right now?

·   Recall a time when you chose wisely.

In this chapter we have studied the ten Personal Foundations from the perspective of how they apply to us personally. By working with each foundation, we can Perceive, Describe, and Accept ourselves in an ever-deepening way.

The current condition of our foundations not only influences our personal lives but also our professional lives. In Chapter 3, we will explore how our Personal Foundations impact our work with our clients.

Foundation Development Plan

The Foundation Development Plan is a way to change ourselves consciously and actively. These exercises are designed to help you to create real steps to take in your change project. You can develop a plan for each Personal Foundation that is unique to you, and you can use any of the exercises to do this.

Exercise 1: Evaluating Foundations

On a separate sheet of paper, write your responses to the questions below for each of the Personal Foundations. Consider this a short brainstorming session, not a lifelong commitment. If you can't do them all now, we suggest making short notes and coming back to them later.

Name of Foundation:

1. What is one aspect of this foundation that I would like to improve?
2. How much do I accept my current condition?
3. Starting with what I know right now, what is something I can do to help me become more conscious of the dynamics of this issue?
4. What agreements or beliefs do I have that influence this issue?
5. Have I tried anything to change this so far?
6. What was the result?
7. If I change this part of me, what will I be like as a result?
8. What kind of help or learning do I need to change this?
9. What plans can I think of right now that might work to implement the change?
10. What will I do as my next step on this project?

Exercise 2: Creating a Foundation Development Plan

This exercise is more detailed and complete than the previous one. Choose one foundation and proceed through the steps.

Step 1: Assess your self by describing the current condition of your foundation, as fully as you are presently aware. Accept yourself throughout this process. Include:

- Stories that demonstrate your foundation. *Example:* Last weekend, when my friends got involved in a political discussion, I could not bring myself to voice my disagreement.

- Does your behavior change according to the circumstance? If yes, in what way?

- How will improvement expand your life?

- Aspects of yourself that you are certain about.

- Aspects of yourself that need further investigation.

- Accept yourself.

Step 2: Make a list of questions to ask to help you learn more.

- Questions to ask your self. *Example:* Am I afraid to disagree out loud? How does this limit my life?

- Questions for others.

- Questions to research.

- Ask lots of questions that include your style, timing, education, and so forth.

Step 3: Observe yourself in action and keep track of what you notice. During this time, do not try to change *anything* until you have spent some time observing and collecting knowledge of the deeper dynamics.

- Use your questions to learn more about yourself as you go about your life in real time. *Sample:* I noticed the other day that I pretended to agree with one of my colleagues. I had a lump in my throat and a burning in the pit of my stomach.

- Continue to accept yourself.

Step 4: Return to your description of your foundation and expand or revise it to include your increased awareness. Continue to practice acceptance.

Step 5: Write a description of yourself as the person you wish to become.

- How would your ideal self behave? *Example:* I would freely and openly debate with my friends and colleagues.

- How would you behave if you completely accepted yourself?

- Clearly articulate your goals.

Step 6: Ask the question: What do I need to know or do that will help me succeed in this change?

- What kinds of techniques have worked for you in the past? *Example:* Role playing has been a powerful tool for me.

- What kind of knowledge or education might be useful?

- Who might help you?

Step 7: What is a reasonable plan to begin your change?

- Keep your timing in mind and build steps into your plan. *Example:* I will set up some role-playing exercises with a friend or coach. Then I will prepare my response for the next time I disagree with someone, perhaps something like "I'm not sure that I feel the same way."

- Accept yourself.

- Remember that your actions are experiments.

Step 8: Act! This means to actually do something differently.

- Decide on the steps of your plan. Then do the first step. *Example:* I practiced role playing with my coach.

- Remain conscious during your experiment.

- Observe your results. *Example:* I feel less intimidated now, and I feel ready to do my next step.

Step 9: Your inventory of the results will begin the cycle again. Your next step might be implemented immediately or revised, depending on the results of your experiment.

You will change as a result of implementing your Foundation Development Plan. Then you will have a new perception and description, which starts you off again. Your plan for change will really have thousands of change cycles within it. They all add up to significant, conscious, active change.

3

How Who We Are Impacts Our Work with Clients

Further Understanding of Foundations

As consultants, we want to achieve excellence. We work hard to deliver results that will truly help our clients. We read books, attend seminars, and work with mentors to continue our professional development. Many of us also cultivate personal development as an aspect of professional growth. In this chapter, we examine how our practice of Perceiving, Describing, and Accepting ourselves affects our client interactions.

Who we are influences not only our personal lives, but is central to the impact we have on our clients. From this standpoint, the Foundation Development Plan presented in the preceding chapter can become an important part of our professional development. What we discover from creating our own plan can be included in our planning with clients, allowing us to capitalize on our strengths and compensate for our weaknesses. We can also learn more about who we are from the results of our client experience.

Each of the Personal Foundations will be revisited here in terms of client interactions, with examples illustrating how the condition of the Personal Foundations impacts clients. The discussion of each foundation will end with exercises that can help to Perceive, Describe, and Accept the current state of our Personal Foundations as they relate to our clients. This process will enable us to broaden and deepen our self-awareness, helping to put it to work for us.

1. Identity

When we are aware of our self in a deep and accurate way, we have a strong sense of identity. What we know or do not know about our self directly affects our client and, of course, our relationship with our work.

We present who we are to our clients through our own view of self. If our view is clear, accurate, and certain, what we tell others (verbally and nonverbally) about ourselves will be congruent with what they observe in our behavior. Additionally, the more conscious we are of our own identity, the more fully we can connect with our clients. If we are hazy in what we know to be true about ourselves, our clients will feel uncertain about what they can expect from us, and this will limit the depth of trust that develops. We will also be more likely to accept projections placed on us by clients.

> I was the first woman to be trained as a T-group facilitator. I trained for eight years before I was given a group to lead. The men in the program were generally trained for one year before they were given a group to lead. I was young and a woman, and National Training Labs (NTL) did not want to lose its reputation by having a young woman running groups.
>
> The most dramatic moment that helped define who I am came from the first T-group that I was able to facilitate. We did the usual opening, which led to a long moment of silence. The silence was broken by a white male who wanted to know what my credentials were for leading the group. This was my greatest fear, because I did not have "credentials" like those who came out of the academic world.
>
> At that moment, I touched my core. I answered that I was in the facilitator role to be helpful and, if at the end I had been helpful, it did not matter what my credentials were. If at the end I had not been helpful, then having credentials would not have made a difference! If he found I was helpful, I had been trained very well.
>
> *Edie Seashore*

Edie's response not only helped her become centered in her own identity, but also increased trust between her and her clients. She called forth her full talent and skill. She remained connected with her own value and her goal of helping the client. If she had reacted by defending herself or trying to convince them of her worth, it would have damaged the foundation of her work with these clients.

> I have been challenged a lot because I was the first woman in the field of OD. I am an ENTJ [on the Myers-Briggs Type Indicator] and naturally rise to leadership wherever I go. I have a good sense of humor, know I am fun to be with, and have wisdom. I have a capacity for sizing things up and zeroing in on what is important. Put that together with a genuine desire to make a difference and you have Edie Seashore, first female president of Antioch College and the first woman president of NTL.
>
> *Edie Seashore*

We can be centered in what we know to be true about our self, while recognizing that new feedback may cause us to revise that or fill in the blanks. Self-identity is a continuous unfolding, a lifelong journey of discovery. Strengthening our self-identity based on accurate self-awareness gives us a solid base from which to act. We are less likely to believe what others say about us without regard to evidence, history, or what we know to be true about ourselves. We can withstand criticism, even unjust or unfounded criticism, without being overwhelmed.

> *As an outside consultant, "Ellen" took a contract to help build the top team of a small, family-owned company. The family owners were in conflict, and the executives responded with a turf war. Ellen is a person who is cheerful, easygoing, and fair-minded, which is one reason the executives chose her to help with this rather messy team. As the team building progressed, conflict heated up and members began accusing each other of being obstructive and territorial. Along with this, two members accused Ellen of taking sides. When she had been new to consulting, this sort of thing had devastated Ellen. Now, however, she was fully confident in her own identity as a fair-minded person. The team members were inviting her to join their conflict, but because she was secure in her identity, she did not have to engage in a war about who she was and what she was like.*

Because Ellen stayed with what she knew to be true about her self, she served her clients well. She didn't join in their pattern of conflict, instead giving them an opportunity to learn another way.

But what if Ellen really had been taking sides, but was not conscious of it? Part of knowing about ourselves includes acknowledging that we have an unconscious. When we receive feedback, we need to remember that all of us have denial systems. Even if we totally disagree with the feedback, we can mentally record it on our feedback scorecard. If we receive similar feedback in the future, we can re-examine its validity. In this way we are continually filling in blanks and making adjustments to our identity as we grow in awareness.

While the results of our work may contain important clues about our identity, our work does not define our identity. In other words, what we are and what we do are not identical.

> During my early years as a consultant with one of the big firms, I had a reputation as the person who could deal with the most difficult of clients. I can tell numerous success stories about how I targeted autocratic company directors and—through personal relationships cultivated during system-wide projects—always, and I mean always, persuaded them that they could get much more out of their workforces by behaving differently. They were usually the CEOs, MDs, or senior operations executives—the ones who could make or break a project. I thrived on this type of situation: The more bully-like the authority figure, the more I relished the challenge of winning him over. (In those days, they were always men.) Some of these directors used their physical presence and assertive/aggressive verbal skills to get what they wanted from their workforces. Others used forms of intellectual bullying, like questioning and challenging everything, emphasizing mistakes, and using performance appraisals in threatening ways.
>
> At some unconscious level, I was finding family members in virtually every client organization that consumed my energy and passion. Because the "autocrats" had allowed me into their organizations, I felt able to challenge them in ways that—as a boy—I wouldn't have dared challenge my father, a multi-skilled bully. When I discovered how powerfully my projections and transferences were motivating me in my work, my attraction to "unreconstructed autocrats" suddenly and completely vanished! I didn't look for them anymore, and I started to say "no" to client opportunities if I didn't want to work with the senior people. The entire focus of my work shifted. I recall feeling very excited and liberated, but also frightened and somewhat depressed

that my self-image and reputation as a successful consultant had been so quickly and completely confounded.

Phil Mix

Who we are may motivate us to practice a certain kind of work. However, if we are conscious of whom we are and what our issues are, we may choose to do our work differently, resulting in work that is more satisfying and fulfilling.

Exercise

In the previous chapter, you considered questions about your personal identity. To see how this foundation impacts your work and your clients, answer the following questions:

- How does the kind of work you do reflect your identity?

- How do you know how your clients perceive you?

- What have you recently learned about yourself during a client interaction?

---

2. Acceptance

When we accept others, we perceive and describe what we observe without ideas about how they ought to be. We may notice that some behaviors are healthier or more functional than others. According to our values, we might hope that someone will change or continue his or her behavior, depending on the impact of it. In practicing acceptance, we are not passive or unemotional, but realistic. Working with the steps of the Active Change Model, including the Accept Step, the choices we make will help change that is more likely to be healthy and functional to occur.

> I was leading a three-day meeting with executives for a client of twelve years. A young, less experienced woman was my contact person at the client site for this meeting. I had offered ideas for the meeting, and she had rejected them as not being what they wanted to do. She was conveying the wishes of her boss, who had told her what to say. I wanted to talk to people and was told that I could not. Partway into the first morning, I said to the senior executive that the meeting was not working and that we needed to stop it. He

agreed, and everyone went home. I was upset with my contact person and called her and chewed her out. I was clear but harsh with her.

Some time later, I received a box of materials I had left at the organization. I put it aside in my office, planning to open it later. Weeks later, I moved it. Months later, I still had not opened it. Almost a year later I thought, "Why have I not opened that box? I cannot open that box. Why?" It was only when I recognized my own failure and let go of the blame I had placed on the contact person that I was able to open the box. I called her and wrote several letters of apology, but never heard from her. I acknowledged the things that I had done that caused that meeting to fail, that I was the primary reason, and I felt cleaner.

At the time, I had no notion of acceptance. I was angry with her; I demeaned her: "This failed because you gave me the wrong information. You are inexperienced." I belittled the experience she had: "It is not your fault you are so inexperienced." I was frustrated.

This experience helped me recognize how protective I am of myself and my reputation and image. To know the extreme that I would go to protect myself—blaming someone else instead of looking at myself—informed me so that I know my vulnerabilities better. Part of my I.D. is that I am too sensitive about my reputation and projected image. That gets in the way of my work.

I was that person before, but this helped to shine light into the corners of who I am. I don't have to announce these parts of myself to others. But I must strive to understand and accept these things about myself. There is a disconnect within myself when I am being the parts of myself that I have not identified and not accepted.

Geoff Bellman

We make judgments about how people should behave to be "right," and when they don't conform to our thinking, they are "wrong." When we apply these "right" and "wrong" standards to our client, we interfere with our clients' change processes. Looking at our own experience, do *we* change because someone else thinks we should? How likely are *we* to change in a way someone else thinks we should because the other person thinks he or she is "right"? How well do *we* change under the guidance of someone who disapproves of us? This may sound obvious, but how often do consultants find themselves saying, "How do I *get them* to. . . ?"

This question is usually asked from a preconceived notion of how clients need to behave in order to succeed in their change efforts.

> *"Aaron" was an internal consultant at a telecommunications company. He described his problem by complaining that his clients wouldn't listen to him. "No matter how I say it or how well I explain it, they just seem to ignore me and do whatever they want. Nobody at this company seems to care enough to apply themselves!" He was thinking of quitting his job and moving on. As we learned more, we found out that he had encountered this problem everywhere he had worked.*
>
> *As we talked, it became clear that he had a very set idea of what his client needed to do. He began with an idea of how things ought to be and how the client ought to work. If the client didn't behave according to Aaron's ideas, the client was wrong. The client was not good enough unless he or she conformed to Aaron's plan. The client would feel this judgmental attitude and would shut down. Because Aaron thought he knew the answers, he neglected to ask his client enough questions to become fully informed. When he realized that all consultants did not share this experience, he began to study his own behavior.*
>
> *He realized that his Personal Foundation in the area of acceptance was not strong, so he created a Foundation Development Plan for himself. This included a number of exercises, questions, and reminders to help him learn to shift from judging to accepting.*

Because Aaron was not accepting of his clients, he was unable to guide them to find their own way to accomplish their goals. When any of us fails to be accepting, our own personal agenda becomes more important than the needs of our clients. At best, we flounder; at worst, we engage in a power struggle. When we accept our clients, we still have goals for the outcome of our work with them, but these goals can be firmly grounded in the real needs of the clients.

These goals might be as follows:

- Our client achieves the goal as he or she has defined it.

- Our process with the client is as healthy and functional as possible, both during the intervention and in the outcome.

- Our client is stronger and more capable of changing and solving problems as a result of the work with us.

- It is the client who chooses from the help we offer.

Although accepting does not mean we are detached or unemotional, we can be *neutral* with our clients. This simply means that we keep our own emotional reactions to the side and out of our clients' way. Some consultants seem to be unaware of becoming emotionally involved during their work. Sometimes they appear to be taking sides within the group, viewing some members as "right" and others as "wrong." At other times, they feel personally challenged by an individual and become emotionally reactive. Aaron, in the example above, felt threatened whenever he was questioned. Instead of remaining emotionally neutral, he would begin to battle with his clients, hoping to "win" and prove himself right. His "help" for them became an arena for him to prove how "right" he was.

When we cultivate *neutrality*, we remember that our agreement is to help our clients. Our own emotional experience is real, but it needs to be kept out of the way of our clients' work. When we set our emotional reactions aside, then our clients have space to do their work with our full attention. Our personal reactions are real enough for us, but they have little to do with working with our clients. It is our job to process our reactions in a separate time and place.

> A few years ago, I was co-facilitating a Future Search conference for a very large corporation. One of the participants was a new director who had just joined the company and had a good reputation for achieving results. He questioned and criticized the process from time to time, but I was able to deal with these situations reasonably well. On the final morning, however, a major challenge arose for me.
>
> I was standing in front of a wall on which the sixty-plus participants had affixed their "what's," "how's," and "unresolved's." The participants were sitting on the floor, in chairs, or standing. As I patiently encouraged the group to sort and cluster their outputs, the new director strode up alongside me holding a sheet of flip-chart paper. On it were four headings that, he said, categorized all of the participants' outputs posted on the wall. He proposed that his headings be used as the basis for forming action-planning groups. I stood silently and imagined that everyone in the room was awaiting my response to him. After a few moments, I asked for other views, but none were forthcoming. Eventually, the managing director, who had played an active part in the process, suggested that we were being a bit "over-consensual." More silence followed. No one spoke in favor of completing the two-and-a-half-day process in co-create mode.
>
> I recall feeling alone and exposed, but not upset or angry. I reminded myself of my role as facilitator. I announced that the group members had to

make a choice: They could complete the co-creation process that had been agreed to before the Future Search and reinforced throughout, or they could stop the process and do something different—perhaps what the new director had suggested. I also said that I considered my contract to be with the full group, so I would respect their decision on how to proceed, but it had to be a group decision, not an individual's. I looked toward my co-facilitator and some of the steering group members, but found I couldn't make eye contact with any of them. More silence. Then, a lone voice from the floor suggested that we finish the co-creation process. One or two others murmured their support. Soon, most of the participants agreed to proceed and we completed the Future Search process.

Since that event, the new director has used several consultants for large and small interventions. He's never asked me to work with him. I have mixed feelings about that, but I can live with it. I believe that before I became aware of how I had been using client authority figures to work issues I had with my father, I would have handled this director's intervention very differently. I imagine that I would have reacted more personally and in a way that would not have served my client's interests.

Phil Mix

All consultants will have this sort of surprise, that is, the client acting outside of the agreement or taking over the agenda during an intervention. Our response will depend on the current condition of our Personal Foundation of acceptance. If we are strong here, we will be more able to remain neutral.

How do we learn to do this? Phil gives us important clues in his stories about acceptance and identity. He had consciously processed his issues with bullying authority figures. He had utilized the help of teachers and therapists. Because of his prior personal development work, he was able to separate whatever his personal reaction to the director was, and this made it possible for him to focus totally on what the client needed at that moment.

Exercise

To help yourself to think about acceptance, remember a time when someone was pressing you to do something "their way," and reflect on the following questions:

- How did you feel?

- What was the outcome?

- How satisfied were you with the outcome?

- How lasting was the change?

- How much did you "own" the outcome?

Now remember a time when someone worked *with* you to achieve a change in your own way, and consider the same questions.

---

3. Agreements

Consciously or unconsciously, we have *agreements* with ourselves about our work, and we also have agreements with our clients. These agreements form the foundations from which we work, including how we work with our clients. A conscious agreement with ourselves is like an inner contract determining the conditions of our participation. We may decide the amount of time or travel that we will put into our careers, what fee structure we need, or what type of clients we are willing to work with. Often the satisfaction we may receive from our work is directly related to these inner agreements. This goes beyond simple attitude to a deeper level of structure and creation.

> As an educator and a feminist, I am very clear that I work for social justice, starting from the inside out. The first contact with a client is blunt enough to establish my stance. I don't care if she likes it or not, because it is an authentic representation of my position. So I don't put money on this interaction— I don't take money for a contract I don't yet understand. It is an investment in setting a decent agreement. I find this is psychologically sound, pragmatic, and practical as a foundation for work contracts. It gives the client a chance to think about it before continuing. Our initial conversation is free-roaming. It lets the client set the agenda.
>
> *Alexandra Merrill*

In this story, Alexandra demonstrates how her agreements translate into a boundary. In both her words and actions she is saying to her client, "Here is the kind of work I do and the style I do it in. Do you agree with me on these parts? If so, we can talk about further agreements."

In Chapter 2, we discussed that, with strong boundaries, we don't arbitrarily change agreements without negotiation. If we cannot negotiate an agreement, then we can at least agree that we disagree in that particular area. This means that all parties are included in any changes.

> *"Ken" is an internal consultant at an agency that supplies reports of environmental data to other companies. He was asked to observe a team and provide feedback to them. The team was a group of experienced people who were experts in their field. They were to meet and contribute their knowledge to the contents of a document. The purpose and agreement of the team was to create joint documents that everyone agreed with and then submit them. "Sally," the team leader, was to write the draft documents for further review by the team. However, Sally repeatedly wrote the documents as a final and submitted them without review by the team.*
>
> *Sally had no boundaries in this area, and this caused a great deal of wasted time and emotional damage with the rest of the team. What she was saying by her actions was that the other team members did not count, she was smarter and better, the time and effort that they had given to the project was useless, and their input wasn't important. Therefore, because she was wiser than all of the other team members, she did not need to comply with the agreements she had made earlier with the rest of the team. When team members complained, she responded by explaining that she was right and they were attacking her.*
>
> *Ken helped the team design and institute a detailed project process plan that was posted and checked off at each stage. He worked with the team to negotiate, clarify, and frequently review their agreements with each other.*

This team had an agreement to include everyone in the product of its project. Sally arbitrarily chose to exclude team members. A healthy agreement is one that *includes* the needs of all parties. For example, someone may have authority to make decisions that affect others. Ideally, the person with the authority will include everyone's needs as completely as possible. And the people affected will have consciously agreed that "Someone needs to be the decision maker here. Even if I disagree with the decision, I will still respect it as being that person's to make."

So when we make conscious agreements, we strive to include everyone's needs. Still, we may unconsciously exclude others or ourselves, or both. When we exclude ourselves, it might manifest as the blank-check syndrome. This is when a consultant is willing to do whatever the client decides is necessary. The consultant has not negotiated any agreement about who does what. When a consultant hands the client a blank check for the project, it means that the client gets to fill in the amount of what the consultant is to give. What the consultant is saying, consciously or unconsciously, to the client is this:

- I will help you regardless of how difficult the job is.
- I will do all the work, even if you don't do your share.
- If the results of our work are not what you desire, it is my fault.
- I can become whoever you need me to be.
- You can change the agreements we have at any time without my involvement.
- I will save you and keep you comfortable.
- I will put in any amount of hours to achieve success by your definition, even if you change that definition.
- I will design and execute the project the way that you want, even if I disagree.
- I will not vocalize any concerns I have about the project because it might jeopardize my role in the project.
- You are entitled to be happy with the outcome, no matter what. If you are not, it is my fault.

This syndrome leads to unhappy clients and exhausted consultants. This is especially common with overly responsible consultants.

> When "Jessica" came to us, she was totally depleted and ready to find another career. She had the "blank-check syndrome" in a big way. She made lavish promises to her clients about what she would do to help them. She neglected to discuss the clients' role in the process, as she imagined that they would naturally follow along. When her projects fell flat, it was generally because the clients were not following through with their end, yet they blamed her. Jessica's expectation was that she would do everything to help them until they were happy. The result of this strategy was that, the harder she tried, the more the clients became dissatisfied.
>
> Jessica made her agreements based on wishful thinking, believing she could create change in people and organizations all by herself. She also made her agreements based on a premise that all the people involved would devote themselves to the project with the same level of commitment and time that she herself had committed. Because Jessica believed that all of the work was her responsibility,

she attracted clients who believed the same thing. She was stunned when she real-
ized what she was doing. Of course! Change involves everyone doing his or her
own part! But what we know to be true and obvious is not always integrated into
our agreements.

Jessica now includes a description of each party's responsibility in her initial
contract with a client. She is in charge of what she will and will not do, not her
client. She has decided that she will not work with clients who do not seem com-
mitted to do their part. With this change, her clients are happier with her and she
is not working nearly as hard as before.

This example demonstrates what can happen when the consultant has not strongly developed the ability to say "no" and feels compelled to say "yes" to most of what the clients want. Changing this is at the center of making a conscious boundary. A boundary is not a wall or a barrier. Actually, with boundaries, there is no need for walls or barriers.

> Getting clear about who I am not relates to the self I am becoming as well as the self I am. There is a built-in "yes" in OD. It means that we are receptive and open toward other people and situations. However, there need to be more built-in "no's." We need to recognize what our boundaries are. Boundaries are not determined by "yes," but by the dynamic between "yes" and "no." The boundary is defined when a "yes" moves to a "no."
>
> *Geoff Bellman*

When we have agreed with ourselves to honor our right to choose, to say "yes," "no," or sometimes "maybe," we can be open with others without being subject to their whims.

Because agreements are so central to the effectiveness of our work and our own level of satisfaction, we will explore them more fully in Chapter 5.

Exercise

To review your agreements about your work and, with your clients, choose a specific situation and spend a moment jotting down answers to the following questions:

- Describe the agreements that are currently in place with my clients, my colleagues, and myself.

- Am I upholding the agreements?
- Have I taken on more than my share of the agreed-on responsibilities?
- Have I left some of my agreed-on responsibilities for someone else to do?
- Whose responsibility is this?
- Is it any of my business?
- Have I been asked to do or say anything?
- Am I respecting the agreements that are in place?
- Am I assuming rather than discussing and negotiating?

4. Integrity

Having high-level integrity means that we consciously choose behaviors that add to the life of everyone and everything. How does our degree of integrity impact our work with clients?

Most consultants would agree that, in essence, our work is a form of service. We are not just making a living—we are helping people to grow and expand. This requires a high level of integrity and a high degree of courage as well.

There are many temptations to give in to whatever the client wants, even if it is not the best solution. Sometimes a client may be uncomfortable with a situation or process. To make the intervention more comfortable may weaken the outcome. At times, it may be appropriate to lean toward client comfort and at other times it may not.

A major consulting firm provided one-on-one coaching for junior executives in a large corporation. The contract the consultants had with the organization provided that the information from the coaching sessions was the "property of the organization." The consultants shared with each other and the senior executives the information they received about what junior executives were experiencing in their work challenges. The corporation used the information gained during coaching sessions to assist in decisions about promotions. Those being coached were not informed about this agreement; there was no discussion about confidentiality with the junior executives.

> *As some of the junior executives found out how information about them was being used, they felt betrayed and lost trust in their coaches and their leaders. However, because it was politically unsafe to "fire" their coaches, individuals in the corporation began to tell the coaches only what they wanted the senior executives or others in the organization to know. Thus, not only was the value of the coaching process lost but, in addition, the behavior of the consultants fostered a practice of deceit within the corporation that would ultimately harm their client.*

In this case, the betrayal was not a direct lie but rather a lie through omission. If our sense of honor is negotiable, it means we carry a belief that people are somehow expendable if it suits us. The result is a crack in the confidence we place in ourselves and in the trust that others place in us. Honest change is much more able to occur within a trusting atmosphere. Change rooted in deceit has an unstable foundation. When change is based on lies or deception, the change is weak, short-lived, and ultimately harmful.

Our clients have entrusted us with their request for help. As the experts, it is our responsibility to decide what might actually help and what might well be harmful. "The work of any professional helper requires the constant exercise of discretion and judgment. The client may not be qualified to appraise the quality of service being offered or the risks involved and, therefore, may have to rely for support and protection on the consultant's standards of conduct" (Lippitt & Lippitt, 1986).

This responsibility of deciding what kind of intervention is healthy or not healthy is a heavy one. Yet it is based on the fact that, ultimately, we are responsible for the outcome of our work. A conscious consultant will learn to predict the probable outcome of any given action. With this knowledge, we consultants can choose our actions according to the result we are seeking. If we are more interested in contributing to healthy growth that includes everyone, rather than short-term selfish interest, then our choices will be guided by that desired result.

> I think about integrity as honesty. The issue of client-consultant honesty is an interesting one. I don't believe that one should be 100 percent honest with clients. There are situations in which a client is not ready to hear the news that she is actually the problem. I may have found information early during the work that led me to that conclusion, but I knew that I could not say it to her then because of the timing. This revelation must come at a time when the client is ready to listen. First, I need to build enough of a relationship so that she would be willing to listen. People who need to hear information such as "You

are the problem" are well-defended, and if I open the barn door too soon, I can't get the message through.

I have had two or three clients who had grandiose dreams about what to accomplish and who also had a fair amount of personal pain. Over time it became clear that they could easily go off the deep end and were using me as an anchor to reality. I did not tell them what to do but acted as their anchor. If I had been completely honest too soon, I would have lost them.

Edie Seashore

When we have strong integrity, we trust ourselves and are consequently trusted by others. With weak integrity, we believe that it is OK to take advantage of others: To steal, lie, or sacrifice others for personal gain and to protect ourselves from pain. Living with integrity does not mean that we adhere to our principles only when it's easy or convenient, but that we put those principles first. Our clients will know that they are honored and valued, and they will be able to transform within that trust.

It helps to be clear about the tenets of integrity that we practice in our professional work. For instance, we might identify one tenet of high integrity as follows: When we do something that matters to others, they have a right to know about it. Another tenet might be to clarify others' assumptions if they appear distorted. Honest disclosure shows our allegiance to our own honor and life-giving behavior.

Exercise

Make a list of your personal and professional tenets of integrity. Then ask yourself, "How completely do I live by these?" For example: I believe in the following:

- Honest disclosure under [fill in what] circumstances.
- When I know that another's assumptions are not accurate, I will clarify under [fill in what] circumstances.
- I will seek to include the best interests of all parties.

Now, write your own code of integrity and keep the list with you when working with clients.

---

5. Authenticity

When we present ourselves authentically, we show who we are to the outside world. If we are authentic with our clients, our behavior will be congruent with what they sense about us. When we are open with who we are, we not only help ourselves, but we help our clients.

If our clients do not trust us, our work with them will be limited. To gain their trust, we first develop trust in ourselves, and then in others. When we are authentic, we set a tone for others to follow. Clients seem to have a kind of radar about this and are usually pretty accurate in their perceptions. If we are not authentic, clients will stay hidden behind their masks. It is as if they say, "You first!" in this regard.

> How do I say "No" to what I am not ready for? This is a good question for young consultants. I don't know of a single client I ever lost by being straight. One of the great gifts that we as consultants bring to the system is a willingness to say, "This is what I am seeing right now. It may not be your truth, but it is what I see." Or even to say something as revealing as, "I am feeling scared, confused, and not sure what is going on right now." Saying what is true for me as a consultant helps others say what is true for them. The old me would have said to myself, "I am confused and I have to straighten it out!"
>
> I take on work because it interests me and I feel centered while I'm doing it. I know I am functioning better when I am straight because my stomach does not get upset. When I need to slow down, my body finds the way to tell me. I have to pay attention to the signals.
>
> *Jane Magruder Watkins*

How do we become more authentic? We may discover that our masks and shields are mostly unconscious, stuck on quite tightly. Becoming more authentic involves more than just approving of the concept. We can begin by making a sustained effort to Perceive, Describe, and Accept who we are as accurately as possible. We can discover this in stages by asking and listening. Then we Perceive, Describe, and Accept our behavior and consider it in the light of our self-identity. How do I know when I am hiding—what does it feel like? Eventually we can make the leap to dropping our masks, even if only a little bit at a time. Each time we do, we notice what happens and decide whether further risk is worth it.

The result of our change toward greater authenticity benefits our clients. This is how we become the change leaders. We change, and that gives permission and encouragement for others to do so. If our clients can become more authentic, their changes will be built on a foundation of truth, not wishful thinking or fantasy. These changes will be integrated and used, not forgotten.

Exercise

Reflect on these questions about authenticity:

- Under what circumstances do I open up more than usual?
- Under what circumstances do I shut down and hide?
- How do I know when I am authentic or not?
- Are there bodily sensations? Am I aware in the moment or later?
- Emotions? Am I aware in the moment or later?
- Thoughts? Am I aware in the moment or later?
- How does my authenticity affect my clients and myself?

---

6. Courage

Change can be scary. Whether large or small, it is still a leap into the unknown. While we may predict that our changes will be good, there is no guarantee. Every change involves risk, and risk brings fear. Our clients hire us to help them change, and even though they want change they are also afraid. We may have watched many clients successfully go down the path of change, and we may feel that this client also will be all right, but the client may feel differently.

Courage is the antidote for fear. Every intervention requires courage, and, as consultants, we practice it routinely. We need it for ourselves to handle the tremors and eruptions of each project, and we also need it to help our clients face their own fears of change. It is hard to imagine having too much courage. Like our other foundations, courage can be intentionally developed. We can practice not hiding from the scary stuff, and in so doing, our courage gets strengthened like a muscle.

Many years ago, I was conducting a training session with a client who was being observed by students from my OD program. We were about halfway through the first morning when a participant said in a loud voice, "What is going on here? Why are we doing this?" I felt she was suspicious of my credibility and credentials and was attacking the program, and I was shocked.

I had an anxiety rush, but I started to "walk toward the problem," which I did physically, talking to her in a quiet, calm voice. I asked her why she was feeling the way she was. I did not try to offer up a fix at that time, but tried to understand how she was feeling. Once I could repeat back how she was feeling and acknowledge that the feeling was in the room, I asked her if we could then continue on with the program. We did and the program was very successful.

At the end of the day, I did a debriefing with the students. They remarked that they would never have thought of "walking toward" the problem in such a physical way. I feel I cannot dare to walk away from strong feelings. I don't have to agree with them, but I need to work with them. This scene has stayed with me for years. I have learned to anchor my feet on the ground and not dodge what is in the room. I do not continue with the program and ignore the issues. That would be disastrous. So I learned a great deal about making a commitment to continue on a courageous path and it worked out as a tremendous learning for me.

Barbara Bunker

Our enthusiasm and commitment to offer the highest service and modeling for our clients will bolster our courage. If we are clear in our agreements with ourselves about who we are and who we are becoming, this will strengthen us, and our goals will become more important than our fears. When the time comes for us to lead our clients through difficult and scary changes, we will have done our homework. We will know personally what it is like to move forward in new ways, and we can provide that knowledge as a structure for clients. We cannot model what we do not have within us. Our clients need courage to implement their changes, and as their guides and change catalysts, we must have our own courage that is strong enough to support theirs.

One night, I got home about 7:30 P.M. and picked up a voice mail from a client apologizing for not meeting me at our 7:00 P.M. meeting. I had forgotten also!

So I called right away and left a voice message saying not to worry and let's reschedule. I then hung up. I said nothing about missing the meeting. A coaching relationship has to be based on truth, and I realized I had told a lie by omission. So I called back and said, "I need to acknowledge what I did not say: That I also forgot about the meeting. I want to apologize for leaving that out of my voice message and for lying to you."

I am not sure how much longer the relationship went on, and I don't even remember if there was any deep connection between the two of us. But I did learn that was an important moment for me to be willing to admit mistakes.

Jim Earley

Exercise

To learn more about your own courage foundation, take a few minutes to write about the following situations:

- A time when your courage served your client well.

- A time when you didn't take a risk but now wish you had.

- Examples of how you exercise your courage in small ways during your work.

- Something scary that you need to do to help your future expand.

---

7. Timing

As consultants, we can practice this mantra: *What is now? What is next? What is now? What is next?* When we are strong in our awareness of timing, we recognize that there are stages to all change. During every process there are steps along the way that always occur. It is like the way a plant grows. We plant the seed in the earth and care for it. We know that it is useless to try to hurry it along, so we enjoy its various stages of growth. We practice *patience*. We might eagerly await its fruit or flowers, but in our wisdom we know that the process is a treasure as well.

As experienced change agents, we are like gardeners. A seedling and a blooming plant require different care. No stage of growth is wrong; it is just the stage that is. Awareness of stages is an awareness of the timing of the process. We help our clients create an environment for transformation. We provide expertise and guidance and stay with them through the stages of the process. Through our experience we know what each stage is like, and that each stage is one more step along the way to the desired outcome. This awareness allows us to guide our clients through each stage without trying to skip steps or rush them along. Just as we know that the stages are predictable, we also know that the amount of time for each stage is not predictable.

> Several years ago, as the connections between my personal work and my work with clients was becoming clearer to me, I was asked by the managing director of a large private health care company to help their managers and staff to identify brand values and to develop service delivery and people strategies in line with those values. I'd known this man for a number of years and he advised me to proceed slowly. He said that he was prepared to invest massive sums in consulting fees to do the project well.
>
> Unfortunately, I was too impatient. My preoccupation with challenging myself to be aware of my reactions to individuals and situations, then to try to name my projections, distorted my judgment about how best to help meet the client's needs. As well as helping them to work on their brand values, I proposed a series of planning meetings and orchestrated interventions, ostensibly aimed at helping people to "understand themselves" and their interpersonal processes within the changing business context. I hadn't contracted at the outset to do this and they weren't ready for it. I was blinded by my own motivation to try out my new learnings about projection in a client setting. I was unaware that I was projecting my need to understand myself onto my client. My colleagues and I were politely asked to withdraw, my self-esteem badly bruised and my consulting firm lamenting a lost opportunity.
>
> *Phil Mix*

Sensitivity to timing offers a real opportunity for consulting excellence. We need to apply our full listening skills to detect clues that reveal the readiness of our clients. Just because we are aware of the next step does not mean a client is ready to take it. We can ask our clients what they have done already and what they think they are ready for now.

> *"Tony" was an outside consultant for a government agency, called in to help a team. Without asking about their timing, Tony spent the entire meeting conducting a needs assessment for the group. The team had already done this and*

was disgusted about having their time wasted. Tony either did not notice the lack of enthusiasm and withdrawn body language, or he chose to ignore it or misinterpret it. No one said anything. When team members were asked later why no one had spoken up, they said they did not know whether Tony was personally connected with their leader, and they were afraid that he would talk about them to the leader if they complained.

In the following story, the consultant didn't have to ask to find out about timing and stages; he listened to the signals and changed direction in an expert way.

The project leader asked "Constantine" to give a presentation to the team and gave the consultant instructions about the help that was needed. Constantine arrived with her prepared presentation, which she then embarked on. However, her planned presentation did not match the step the team needed to be doing at that time. As people began to ask questions, Constantine noticed the gap and smoothly transitioned the agenda to the current need. She was able to make the transition in such a way that nobody realized it wasn't the original agenda. The team was expertly guided through their current stage of work and received the prepared presentation at a later meeting.

When the situation is right, the apparently magical leap to change occurs. Transformational interventions occur when all of the preliminary steps are taken in their own time. It is like the sudden unfolding of a flower. Or it is like being sure to include all the ingredients in a recipe. We can bake the cake before it is mixed, but it will just be hot flour and milk. As consultants, we learn recipes for intervention. When we are skilled, we use the recipes with care and attention to their unique timing.

Exercise

To measure your own sensitivity to timing, consider the following questions for a client you are working with:

- What has the client accomplished so far?
- What does it seem that the client needs as a next step?
- Is the foundation in place for this?
- Does the client need a push now, or more gentle leadership?

---

8. Knowledge

The knowledge that we have is one of our most important tools. We have knowledge about life in general and knowledge about our professional practices. We also have knowledge about how to apply our tools. Our clients hire us for all of this knowledge—it is the expertise we have to offer.

The more diverse tools that we have to use in our interventions, the more choices we have. The old adage, "When all you have is a hammer, everything begins to look like a nail," is completely true. The more experience, education, and creativity that we incorporate within ourselves, the greater are our capabilities. Techniques can be learned or invented, and the more the better. The fact that we have utilized a technique and it has worked well does not prove its future value. Each circumstance is new, and the more tools we have and know how to use skillfully, the better.

There are established techniques for interventions and solving problems. Many of these are like a recipe in a cookbook—when we follow the recipe, we are likely to get similar results every time. However, people are not as predictable as food. The difference between a great chef and an adequate cook is in the ability to improvise and treat each dish as unique.

> I rely on informed instinct. Knowledge is very important to that. Clients hire us because of knowledge. They are attracted to what we know, so we have to have a base of expertise, models, concepts, and experience. So the clients are attracted, but that is not why they stay. They stay with me because I have the confidence to use my instincts. I interpret and make leaps from what I know to what I guess or believe.
>
> When I was less experienced, I put considerable time into building up my toolkit in a how-to way. Then I moved beyond that into designing tools and creating models and concepts about what works in organization change. Along the way, I over-valued technique. I would say, this is a gift to mankind and everyone needs to do it. I believed in it too deeply. I accepted techniques as values, rather than just methodologies. With time, I built models so that techniques could be used within them.
>
> *Geoff Bellman*

We have three main ways to gain the knowledge to be successful consultants: education, experience, and creativity. Formal education will provide the theoretical framework for what we know and do. This can come from university courses, specialized curricula, or certification programs. We can also learn from mentors, colleagues, books, and seminars. Experience and creativity help us to build "informed instinct" that can sometimes produce what seems like a simple intervention at the time, but that leads to a huge organization change.

> Once I was working with a bunch of guys, older white guys, forty or fifty of them. We were meeting with the executives and talking about the directions that they wanted to take the company. The CEO had notions about what he wanted, and he wanted to engage these guys while being consistent with his hands-off leadership style. He wanted the group to come up with what it would take to change the system. In the middle of the discussion, I got an idea. I had not planned it, but I have used this method often:
>
> Ask everyone to stand up and pair up with someone they know less well. Then ask them to ask these questions of each other:
>
> - What do you do?
> - Why is that important to you?
> - Why is that important?
>
> In eight or ten minutes, there was a lot of good energy and discussion in the room. When I stopped them after they had interviewed each other, I asked, "How did that go?" One guy said, "I bet I haven't talked about that in twelve years." Others said, "I didn't know you thought about stuff like that!" This spontaneous exercise led to a large-group intervention that Kristine Quade did with the entire organization.
>
> It was a great surprise to all of us. Most of my best work is not planned. I don't know what was going on before that, but I sensed we needed to tap into a level that was there but unacknowledged and important.
>
> *Geoff Bellman*

In the authors' experience, consultants who are successful and have an expanding business practice are also constantly engaged in learning more. There appears to be a strong correlation between the personal expansion of knowledge and the professional expansion of one's business.

Exercise

To assess your current level of knowledge, consider these questions:

- How do you learn to enhance your ability to work with your clients?

- How can you tell when you need to learn more in a particular area?

- What do you say when asked to do something you know nothing or little about?

- Does it seem as if your clients perceive you as knowledgeable?

---

9. Communication

Communication is based on sharing. We share what we know and who we are with others. We listen to others to receive what they share with us. This may sound simple enough, yet few people are masters. Simple is not the same as easy.

> We worked with a new company that was the result of a merger of four companies—two European and two North American. We facilitated a large-group intervention around people's expectations of the new company. The purpose of the meeting was for everyone to work together to discover and express their thoughts. One of the company's internal consultants, "Julia," was a participant. Everyone was seated at tables of eight. However, Julia dominated her table. She seemed to think that she was supposed to take over and tell everyone else at her table what to think and do. Her table mates were silent and resentful. The people at other tables were having animated discussions, bouncing each other's ideas back and forth. Julia did not seem to notice any of this, but her table mates did. This consultant conducted conversations by talking "at" people, not sharing with them or listening to them.
>
> *Kristine Quade and Renée M. Brown*

If we want to be effective in helping others to change, we need to learn to share what we know in an appropriate degree and manner, and to listen fully. This kind of communication strengthens participants and builds bridges.

I let other people choose the direction, instead of imposing my direction. I rely on questions to help them come to their own insights. This deepens their self-knowledge and commitment to growth. That is the difference between the guru pontificating versus the truth coming from the individual. My role is to help them discover something that was there but previously unseen.

Ken Hultman

Sometimes we may notice that something odd is happening, but we don't ask about it. We just plow forward, hoping that whatever it is either comes out or goes away. Usually that may not be the best strategy. When we don't really know what is going on with someone, we can't really chart an effective course.

I remember starting a Monday morning session for a group comprised of school superintendents. I was co-facilitating with a colleague. We knew the people had met on Sunday night. Early in the morning, we examined the four frames for looking at organizations. About an hour and a half into the presentation, we took a break. My colleague and I felt that either this was a strange group because there was a flat affect with no response, or something was going on that we did not know about. We were concerned because some of the participants were mildly hostile, and some had completely bailed out and were not even mentally present.

After break, we said, "We need to talk about what is happening in this group. This feels different. Is there something we need to know about?" They told us that during the weekend, one member had had a serious allergy attack and because the rescue service was not able to get there rapidly, he had almost died. The whole group had been traumatized by what had happened. There was a huge psychological impact on the group, and they had not talked about it or voiced how they felt or dealt with their own fears. So we stopped to talk about it. Eventually we asked, "Do you want to go on or discontinue the program?" They gave us the answer to move on.

It is important not to ignore what is happening with the system. It takes courage because it moves the consultant and the clients into a high period of uncertainty.

Barbara Bunker

When we communicate, we can only share from where we are. We speak from our own frames of reference, and we listen from our own frames of reference. If we ignore this, we might imagine that we understand and are understood, but we probably are not correct. Sometimes it's possible to learn to speak or to listen in order to account for the differences. Other times, we have to work hard to translate into our own frame of understanding.

> I once taught groups of high-level managers of agriculture. We spent six to eight weeks as a team learning about project management and organization development. I would say, "I am American and what you will hear from me is the Western view of how things work. I will share that with you so that you can understand how we think and work. Your job is to take what I share and make it useful in your culture. A lot of what I want to do is share with you, and then you share how it is useful, what you would have to change to make it useful." This worked in the teaching environment and is now working for me in my consulting environment.
>
> *Jane Magruder Watkins*

When we listen fully, we put our private stuff aside for later and give our full attention to what is happening in the present moment. Our agreement to help our client means that we are there for him or her. We are fully present to listen with heart, mind, and ears to the business at hand. Our client will then be spared from having to suffer from our personal projections and inner static.

Exercise

To assess your level of communication with your clients, consider these questions:

- What do you feel like inside when you are fully listening to a client?

- How do you feel when someone is "talking at" you?

- How do you know when your client really hears and understands what you have said?

---

10. Wisdom

Wisdom is the crown of excellence. When we are wise, we are conscious and present. We incorporate what we have learned and experienced. We blend all of what we are and know into the choices we make. Having wisdom is having a presence of self and at the same time being aware and connected with others in a full way. Everyone benefits from choices grounded in wisdom, because they are inclusive and compassionate.

> I have gone through a big business shift that was triggered when my wife was diagnosed with cancer. We stepped back to look at our lives to see what life we wanted to live. What keeps me going is that I have a vision of "a better life," which is a rich tapestry of multiple dimensions of what a better life looks like.
>
> As I practice making the choices, it gets easier. If in fact I am able to see the fork in the road, recognize it, and be conscious about it, I can check it against who I want to be. It is the same question I ask my clients about their preferred futures and what is going on right here and right now. I ask myself how I would be doing business now, who I would be paying attention to, and what I can bring of that into the present. I know that what gets paid attention to gets done.
>
> I see myself honoring who I am and what is important to me.
>
> *Robert "Jake" Jacobs*

Wisdom is not something we are born with or simply given—it is developed. We develop it by expanding our consciousness and embodying change. We learn to be conscious of the many dimensions of interactions. We learn to include others in our choices. We help people find and follow their own paths, not those we invent for them. We help our clients learn to be self-sufficient, courageous, and wise themselves. And we continue to develop ourselves as human beings by practicing continuous self-change. When we have developed real wisdom, we will have something of exceptional value to offer to our clients.

> I once interviewed for consulting work with the Defense Mapping Agency. After the preliminary interview, I was scheduled to meet with the major general. As I entered the boardroom for my interview with the major general, I found myself in a room full of men. As the major general entered, all the men stood. He said, "I am late, but I had salad for lunch and I had a bit stuck in my teeth. And I had to get it out." I was the only one who responded, and I told a story about the time I and my husband, Charlie Seashore, had attended a faculty meeting at which the dean of academics at Fielding had something

in her teeth and no one let her know it. I then said, "Why don't we want to give feedback, even when it informs someone of something they'd like to know?" The major general then told a story about the time that his fly had been open and no one had told him.

So now I knew he liked stories. Whenever I could see what he was talking about, I would tell a story from my professional background, mentioning the name of the client as a way of conveying my experience. At the end of the interview, I was asked if I had any questions. I said, "This is your last assignment with the Air Force and you would like to leave a legacy. So when do we start?" His response was "That will do," pointing to me and indicating I had just been named the consultant.

This relationship continued for many years. I understood him and he understood me. But people below him were trying to protect him. They would give me advice about what would or would not work. I wanted to do an Open Space and was told, "It won't work." But when I ran it by the major general he said, "If you think it will work, then do it." I learned that if I had clarity about what I could do and what would work, then he would support me.

The issue of giving feedback came up again when I was working with the team and the major general decided to give feedback. He started with one man whom he did not particularly like and gave him strong feedback. Then he moved to the second person, whom he clearly liked, and gave him great feedback. I had a hunch, which was followed by feeling flushed, hot, and afraid of the clarity that came to me. So I asked the major general to stop for a moment and I said, "You asked me to stop you when I could help. I think it would help for the members of your team to give feedback to you."

"Great!" he said, and started with the person he liked. I stopped him and asked him to go back to the first team member, who proceeded to blast the major general. The major general was stunned, and after a moment of silence he said, "Shame on you for not being straight with me, and shame on me for letting this go on so long. I did not realize I had hurt you so deeply."

At this moment we had come to the end of the time for the meeting, and I had to make a dash for the airport. I was upset with myself because of the interaction and worried that we should have done this activity sooner so there was time to bring closure. The next day I called to see whether anyone was still speaking to me! I was told, "This was the breakthrough we needed." It turned out that the first man could now retire with dignity because he was able to say what he needed to say, and the major general was able to demonstrate what he needed in terms of feedback. It was one of my greatest interventions because I did not back away from it!

Edie Seashore

Exercise

Remember a time when you chose wisely during a client intervention. The incident may or may not be dramatic. Remember what you did and how you did it.

Repeat this exercise frequently. When we remember what and how we did something, no matter how insignificant, we are anchoring ourselves to what we already know and putting it to use for the future.

Foundation Development Plan

These exercises will be similar to those in Chapter 2, but applied to your client experience.

Exercise 1: Evaluating Foundations as They Impact Clients

On a separate sheet of paper, write your responses to the questions below for each of the Personal Foundations in light of your work with clients. Consider this a short brainstorming session, not a lifelong commitment. If you cannot answer them all now, make short notes to come back to later.

Name of Foundation:

1. How does this foundation affect my client work?
2. How much do I accept my current condition?
3. Starting with what I know right now, what is something I can do to help myself to become more conscious of the dynamics of this issue?
4. What agreements or beliefs do I have that influence this issue?
5. Have I tried anything to change this so far?
6. What was the result?
7. If I change this part of me, how will my client work change?
8. What kind of help or learning do I need to change this?
9. What plans can I think of right now that might work to implement the change?
10. What will I do as my next step on this project?

Exercise 2: Creating a Foundation Development Plan for Work with Clients

Choose something that happens during your client interactions that concerns you. Proceed through the steps below.

Step 1: Describe the pattern that concerns you, as fully as you are presently aware.

- Describe the client's pattern of behavior. *Example:* My clients don't seem very forthcoming.

- Describe your pattern of behavior. *Example:* I am somewhat secretive (foundation: authenticity)

- Accept your client and your self.

- How do you think your pattern of behavior impacts your clients?

- How does your pattern impact your performance?

Step 2: Generate questions to ask that will help you investigate the situation more fully.

- Questions to ask your self. *Example:* How does my behavior contribute to what I experience here? Do these events remind me of other events in my personal history?

- Questions to ask of others: Feedback from clients, colleagues, mentors.

- Questions to research: Books, stories, etc.

Step 3: Observe clients you are currently working with.

- Generate questions that will help you become more conscious of the client's pattern and culture.

Step 4: Use self-observation during work with clients. Use the knowledge gained from the above steps to become conscious of the pattern in real time. Continue to accept yourself and your clients.

- Identify the methods and circumstances during your work that you will use to extend your awareness of how this occurs in action. *Example:* I will watch to see what cues I may be giving about my trustworthiness. Do I gossip about other clients? Am I listening well? Am I asking enough questions?

- Develop questions to ask of your self or others to dig deeper in your quest. *Example:* Who seems to be forthcoming with me? Who doesn't? Is there something I do that is different in these cases?

- Continue to fill in the blanks with self-observation questions and their answers. *Example:* Is this a problem in some circumstances more than others? Am I secretive? What are my personal beliefs about openness? Is there a particular kind of information the client seems reluctant to share?

Step 5: Describe the consultant you are, and the consultant you are becoming.

- Through questions, discover and decide on the consultant you are becoming. *Example:* What would my ideal self behave like? How would I be able to help my clients?
- What kind of relationship do you want to develop with your clients?
- Clearly articulate your goals.

Step 6: Create your action plan.

- What are reasonable steps to begin your change?
- What kinds of techniques have worked for you before?
- What help or education might be useful?
- Ask lots of questions to include your style, timing, education, etc.
- Remember, it usually costs more to not ask a question than to ask it.
- Develop as many steps as you can or wish to. *Example:* I am more secretive than I want to be. This seems to influence my clients. During client interactions, I will make efforts to share more of myself as well as volunteer more information about the project. I may intimidate people when I ask them questions. I will experiment with different attitudes, such as curiosity or deeper interest when I ask questions.
- You may have several plans to work on one project.

Step 7: Act: Do the steps that you have outlined. The action will be new; the results will give you new knowledge.

You will change as a result of implementing your Foundation Development Plan. Then you will have a new perception and description, which starts you off again. Every time you change, your relationship with clients will change. Over time, your work outcome will change dramatically.

4

Opening the Doors of Change with Questions

Active Change Is Not a Haphazard Process

Active change comes about by moving through specific steps. The initial steps identified in the Active Change Model are *Perceive, Describe,* and *Accept.* Chapter 2 explored the intricacies of these steps applied to ourselves, and Chapter 3 explored them related to clients. Work with these preliminary steps lays the groundwork for the next step: *Question.*

Questions are central to the Active Change Model because this is how we become conscious of more relevant data on which to base our solutions. As consultants, it is our responsibility to discover the intentions and mental pictures that are present when we interact with clients. Questions help us to see change through the clients' eyes and to dig deeper for more data. We cultivate an awareness of the whole situation, and this enables us to choose the best action possible from the available options.

Developing and asking effective, insightful questions is an art that we can become more skillful at, whatever our present stage of ability. Our skill in developing and asking questions is a barometer of our creativity. When this skill is developed, we avoid getting stuck in loops, asking the same questions over and over again and getting the same answers. We can tap into the creativity of both the person asking and the person answering, helping to change perceptions so that issues are seen in new ways and a wider variety of solutions become visible. We can learn from the answers to our questions, but we can also learn from how we formulate the questions and from the impact they have.

One excellent way to develop the skill of questions is to practice on ourselves. We can question ourselves about our lives and study how we formulate the questions and the kinds of answers they bring up. We can see how questioning enables us to view our lives in new ways, and we can become more deeply aware of the power and possibilities of the process of questioning. For example, consultant and teacher Alexandra Merrill has used the following questions in her self-discovery process:

- What am I here on the planet to accomplish?
- What is my understanding of the prejudicial nature of the human mind?
- How can I do my work and do no harm?
- Why am I wearing a female body on this round?
- What is the ethical practice of female authority?
- What is the impact of my whiteness on my work in the world?
- What is the relationship of my sexual orientation to my work in the world?
- How can I behave in a compassionate way in all my interactions?
- How do I live my understanding of the principles of interdependence?
- How am I complicit in perpetuating the suffering of others?
- How has my being a mother, a daughter, and a sister had an impact on my work in the world?

Gathering Data

As consultants, we have been trained to develop and use questions when we enter a system to help us gather information, which can then be fed back to help the system see itself. We develop questions that help us to understand what is going on so we can effectively recommend the appropriate intervention to the client. We pose these questions with the purpose of "gathering data."

If our goal is to promote active change, we want the data-gathering process to be guided by as much awareness as possible. There are two aspects to this: The *conscious consultant* and the *conscious question.*

The Conscious Consultant

As consultants, we enter into the process of questioning with a certain amount of awareness of what is around us. If we are not aware, we cannot see opportunities to pose questions that have impact. The opportunities may be there, waiting for us to see them, but if we are not in a conscious state, we may overlook what is right in front of us. In Chapter 2, we examined our Personal Foundations and worked with the Foundation Development Plan, developing our awareness of ourselves as a necessary component in being awake to ourselves and our surroundings. In Chapter 3, we looked at how consciousness of our foundations applies to the work we do with clients. All of the work of Perceiving, Describing, and Accepting that we have done in our relationship to ourselves and our clients contributes to our being *conscious consultants,* and we can then bring this aspect of awareness to the data-gathering process.

The Conscious Question

The other important aspect we can bring to the process is the *conscious question,* to which the rest of this chapter is devoted. We, the authors, have identified seven *dimensions* that are at the core of conscious questions. Although there may be others as well, these seven seem essential to creating conscious, impactful questions, which can then lead to conscious actions. The dimensions are brought into play by the conscious consultant who is formulating and asking the questions. It is important that the consultant internalize the dimensions in order to develop the skill of developing and asking conscious questions. See Figure 4.1.

Figure 4.1. Questions with the Seven Dimensions Are the Key to Change

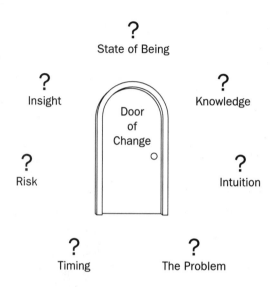

The seven dimensions are as follows:

1. *State of Being:* The Seeker on a Quest.

2. *Knowledge:* What We Know or Don't Know.

3. *Insight:* What Does the Question Really Mean?

4. *Intuition:* Now Where Did That Come From?

5. *Risk:* Willingness to Lance the Wound.

6. *Timing:* Now Is the Only Time There Is.

7. *The Problem:* Will the Real Problem Please Stand Out?

Dimension 1: State of Being: The Seeker on a Quest

Meaningful questions come from deep within ourselves. They take on the nature of our state of being as we enter the questioning process. As such, our initial questions lay the groundwork for the degree of awareness that will be present in the subsequent questions we develop.

> There are times when I am at a party or a meeting and I just don't want to be there. So when I meet people, I ask them superficial questions like, "What do you do?" or "Where do you work?" This comes from my own energy of not wanting to be in this place at this time. There are other times when I am in an open, curious, and active state, where I really do want to connect with people, and I will ask questions from that state, such as, "Why is that important to you?" or "Can you help me to understand your point?" I am always amazed at the difference in my perception of the party or the meeting. I am aware that it all starts with my own state of being.
>
> *Kristine Quade*

Being in an active, participatory mode when questioning brings the process alive. Four qualities help us to open to this way of being when asking questions. These are *acceptance, seeking, curiosity,* and *courage.*

Acceptance

Acceptance is to have an open mind about what is presenting itself. An open mind is one that sets aside judgment. There is an acknowledgment that we are not sure of the way things are, and we are then able to look for alternatives. When we are accepting, we do not rely on preconceived notions about what we think the answer is or should be. We let go and open to what is new and look with fresh eyes.

Seeking

When *seeking*, we are not content to rest with preconceived notions but are searching for what is as yet unknown. Like a dedicated scientist, we become aligned with a desire to know the fullest level of truth possible, and that becomes more important than our personal agenda or ego. In seeking, we never imagine that we already know the answer when we ask a question. The question really *is* a question, and we listen intently to the answer. Then, whatever answer arises will be new because of our state of being.

I am driven by a passion to know myself. I work at it until I see it. I can identify it to me, to you, and to the world. At each of the stages of searching or
practicing Action Research with myself, if I can't get the answer, I continue to
gather data and then suddenly *here I am*!

Kathy Dannemiller

Curiosity

Curiosity is a state of being awake to and interested in new possibilities. We look
from a fresh perspective to be able to see what may have been present all along, but
has gone unnoticed. For example, as humans continue to learn about outer space,
we become aware of what has always been there but has been invisible to our ways
of seeing. The dimension of space has now shifted for us. As our technology
improves, so does our understanding of what has been with us all along. Without
curiosity, we would not be able to discover previously unseen realities.

Curiosity is the foundation of questions for me. It is where the questions
percolate. The places that trip me are when I get into the expert mode or when
I focus on what I am "supposed" to know. When I am asking myself what I
should know, then I am feeding the old story. When I lose my way in coaching, I go back to curiosity. Curiosity helps me to lead clients to their own
stories.

Kim Marshall

Courage

Courage supports our willingness to face difficult situations and consider questions
that challenge the status quo. There are questions that take courage to put to our
clients—what coach Kim Marshall calls "jaw-dropping questions." There are questions that take courage just to formulate, when we challenge beliefs, attitudes, and
knowledge simply by considering the question. The degree of courage that is present as we come to the questioning process reflects the courage that we have developed as one of our Personal Foundations.

Our state of being is always present in the questions we consider, as well as in the
questions we fail to develop and put forward. To be aware of our state of being as we
develop questions contributes to the questions themselves being *conscious* ones. The
example that follows shows how the qualities of acceptance, seeking, curiosity, and
courage come together to create a state of being that creates conscious questions.

"Evelyn" began to notice a repeating pattern in her consulting work. Although she wanted her client to achieve a glorious breakthrough, it wasn't happening. Just about the time she began to think, "Wow! They're really ready to go for the gusto and dramatically transform," her client would begin to waffle and take some kind of sideways route. Evelyn began to see this pattern after she developed a strong desire to know what was really going on and whether she had a role in the process. She sincerely wanted to know the truth, regardless of how uncomfortable the answers might be.

First, she focused on her own attitude of acceptance. She began by listing her preconceived notions of what she thought might be happening to bring about this barrier to change. Then she put her list aside so she could look further as the seeker. She developed and asked questions and made observations to receive more data. She found herself wondering whether the recurring events happened just because that is how people are or whether they had anything to do with her own unconscious behavior.

She noticed that as she became more curious through her questioning process, she was able to observe more about what was going on, both with herself and with her clients. This opened up broader perspectives for her to consider, and this required courage.

Her state of being, then, was at the core of the conscious questions she developed:

- *What seems to happen during my work with clients?*
- *Can I fully describe what is occurring?*
- *In what other circumstances have I experienced this same story?*
- *How would I describe the pattern?*
- *What are my assumptions about what is going on?*
- *What kind of emotional charge do I have around this?*
- *Does this seem to happen the same way with other consultants?*
- *Does this happen with all my clients?*
- *What is going on with me when I have this experience?*
- *Is there a repeatable pattern of mine that I can see that is the same as the client's?*
- *If I were a curious scientist, how would I explore this situation?*

- *What can I learn if I look at this situation as if it were a picture to learn from?*

- *Can I set aside my investment in the situation to wonder about what is going on?*

- *Where is the fear in me? In my clients?*

- *Has this always happened this way? What has changed, if anything?*

- *Do I really want to know the truth of this dynamic?*

- *How will I, and how will my client, benefit from knowing the cause of this dynamic?*

- *Do I have any resources available that might help me in my search?*

Dimension 2: Knowledge: What We Know or Do Not Know

A good question depends in part on basic knowledge. An accountant is prepared by his or her training to ask innumerable questions about a company's finances that, say, a biologist would never think of. The more we know, the more the questions we ask will be meaningful. As consultants, we know about change because we have studied the theory and application of change processes. We have continued to learn about business, trends, technology, people processes, and so forth. This might be called our "head" knowledge.

We also have "heart" knowledge, which comes out of our experience. It is how we put our head knowledge to use. As we experience conscious, planned, and active internal change, we learn about human development in a way that goes beyond conceptual understanding. Our experiences and what we have done to integrate them magnify the knowledge base we have. With a rich knowledge of human dynamics gained through personal experience, we can ask insightful questions that address levels that we would not even know existed without that experience. Continuing to learn more about both the external and the internal environment expands what we know. The more we know, the more we can ask.

At the same time, a good question requires that we be able to *suspend* what we know or think we know. We have our biases, assumptions, personal agendas, mindsets, and blind spots. Because we never really know the absolute truth, we must be willing to set aside what we already know when a new piece of information comes in. The seeming paradox is to be in a state of both knowing and not knowing. In other words, "I know what I know until I have new information." We have to be able to keep going without a complete answer.

Robert Boostrom (1996), in his book *Developing Creative and Critical Thinking*, has this comment about knowledge and discovery: "A good way to stay out of the rut of taking things for granted is to ask questions. Another way of putting it is that reflection demands curiosity. When your curiosity leads you to start asking questions, then your mind has something to work on" (p. 6).

One valuable way to expand our knowledge is to actively seek out viewpoints that are likely to challenge accepted and comfortable perspectives. We humans are lovers of comfort, and we like to have our own opinions supported. We often seek advice from those who are likely to agree with us. Like children, we seek out the person most likely to give us the answer we want. We find differences of opinion uncomfortable, yet it is just this sort of conflict that can generate a lot of creativity.

The following questions help us to think about how we deal with conflicting information:

- What do we usually do when we come across data that seems to conflict with what we know?

- How likely are we to follow the conflicting data wherever it leads?

- Do we tend to be skeptical of the source of the new data, preferring to believe data that agrees with our preconceived notions?

Developing skillfulness in asking excellent questions requires that we learn to be suspicious of our assumptions and guarded against complacency, realizing that these are deadly to creativity. An open mind wants truth more than it wants comfort.

Good questions lead to answers that lead to more good questions. This is a key to healthy change. Our question process keeps us seeking to know the validity of the answers that arise. When we plan the change process, we can use the following questions to increase our awareness of the nature of the data:

- Is the data verifiable fact, or is it opinion, assumption, or consensual agreement?

- Does the client system tend to seek and accept the word of the leadership without question?

- Does the client system tend to put a spin on the word of leadership?

- In what ways do the members of the client system seek to challenge information?

While we use what we know—the answers to our questions—we continue to ask more questions. This is what is meant by living in the state of the question, where an answer to a question is never final but only an experience on the way to a new question. We ask every question as a new question, even ones we may have asked many times before. Because all things change and each moment is new, each time we ask a question the answer will be a little different. Sometimes, a familiar question will bring a surprising and new answer. With this attitude, we can discover both what we know and what we do not know.

Dimension 3: Insight: What Does the Question Really Mean?

There are four parts to discovering what a question really means:

1. *The construction of the question.* A question holds its own meaning. There is a literal meaning: "What time is it?" contains the quest for what time it is now.

2. *The energy behind the question.* The energy driving the question may only become apparent in person rather than in print. For example, the person asking, "What time is it?" might need to know the time or be using the question as a reminder.

3. *The awareness inspired by the question.* By being asked this question, the person with the watch may be triggered into thinking that it is time to go home, that time is important, or that it is annoying when people ask what time it is!

4. *The assumptions within the question.* The question "What time is it?" carries assumptions, such as that the person being asked has a watch, knows how to tell time, can determine what time it is, and has the accurate time.

The first three elements of a question might all be influenced by the fourth element: *assumptions.* Because this fourth element is so powerful and interwoven in the other three, it is important to understand the complexities that might surface.

As consultants, we need to be keenly aware of how our assumptions drive the real meaning of the questions we ask. We need to be conscious not only of the literal meaning of the words but also of what they imply. Consider the difference between "What is wrong with you?" and "What is happening with you right now?" The first is posed as a question but includes a judgment, while the second suggests an interest that is spacious and accepting. To be able to deal effectively with assumptions we must be conscious of the ones we make, and this requires an attitude of seeking. Seeking helps us to explore our assumptions continually as we generate questions.

Every question contains assumptions. To bring those assumptions into the light, we might ask the following questions:

- What does this question assume to be true?

- What does the wording of the question imply?

- Is the question designed to lead to an answer that we have already decided on?

Asking these questions is like making a request of an inner librarian who hunts down the answer and uploads it into awareness. Checking assumptions is like running a screening check on our level of consciousness. We can continue to examine our assumptions by asking:

- What is my belief about this question?

- Where did that belief come from?

- What answer am I looking for?

- How does this answer correlate with everything else I know?

- Am I looking for data that confirms what I know?

- Am I looking for data that challenges what I know?

- Where did I get this information?

- Do I need to run a reality check with someone?

When we gather information from an outside source, we can also be on the look-out for incorrect assumptions by asking:

- What is the source that we are receiving this information from?

- How reliable, educated, and opinionated is the source?

- How crucial is the information we are seeking?

- What will happen if this information is wrong?

To illustrate how assumptions are present in questions whether we are aware of them or not, several questions are provided below, along with their underlying assumptions. By paying attention to the assumptions within the question, we can find gateways to new and unexpected dimensions to explore.

How can I become more creative? This implies:

- There is an "I."
- I can become more creative.
- There is a way to become more creative.
- I am already creative.
- The answer will be useful to me.

How am I holding myself back? This implies:

- There is an "I."
- I am in fact holding myself back.
- I am conscious of holding myself back, but not of how I am doing it.
- The answer will be useful.

Have I already decided, consciously or unconsciously, what is the cause of the problem that I am facing now? This implies:

- There is an "I."
- I might or might not have decided.
- There is a problem.
- It is a problem that I face now.
- There is a cause.
- It is important to know what the cause is.
- I might have decided unconsciously, without examination or debate, what the cause is.
- An unconscious decision about the cause may be different from a conscious one.
- I may have consciously decided, but not realized the meaning of it.
- If a decision is already made, it is important to name it as such.
- It is important to determine how a decision might have been made.
- I may want to examine previous conclusions about my method and source of data.

Our assumptions can get us stuck in the rut of same old questions leading to same old answers. Sometimes getting outside of our assumptions is the hardest work of all!

> I learned that I can make assumptions or I can seek to understand. When I walk into a system, there is a change in the reality of both myself and the system. I can stand in the client system in ignorance, or I can stand there in my own reality, which may change their reality. I don't believe we can ever objectively know what is going on. I believe there is no such thing as an objective observer. The act of observing changes the thing that is being observed. The idea of being an "objective observer" is a myth, because I am still putting myself in judgment of the system. When I walk into the room, I am now a part of the system. The task is to not take my knowledge into the system, but for me to work with the system so that we can all grow and change. I see myself as helping to create a crucible for change. I try to understand how they see the system and they try to understand how I see the system, and then we can both grow and change.
>
> *Jane Magruder Watkins*

Dimension 4: Intuition: Now Where Did That Come From?

Because every question is an experiment, there is some level of "gut" that is involved with the question. Questions may form in our minds without our knowing where they came from. But when one persists, we may ask the question aloud and discover that we have opened a doorway into a profound new awareness for our client. In cultivating our intuition, we can practice paying attention to the urgings and hints we get from within. Then we can ask ourselves, "How did I know that? Where did it come from? How was I able to contact it?"

> When I am coaching, it feels like questions just come. As questions emerge, sometimes I think, "Gosh, am I supposed to ask that question?" My job is to be willing to go into that territory—and not to second-guess. I think we are intuitively afraid to ask a question that may take us to totally new places. To do so risks opening the mindset we are working in. By agreeing to surrender, to be truly lost, we help ourselves—and our clients—to find the place where possibility lives.
>
> *Kim Marshall*

It is important that we begin to rely on these sixth-sense questions as important avenues to knowledge for ourselves. We all have internal libraries that are vast resources. In them is stored all of our knowledge and experience, including the parts that we have forgotten. Our intuition makes it possible for us to access these internal libraries and bring up something that is hidden from our present knowing. When we listen to our inner librarians, we are accessing powerful parts of ourselves.

> I once worked with a man that I did not like. I worked genuinely hard to generate good feelings about him. He was not a terrible man, but a difficult one. I was brought in to do team building and I could understand how the group was feeling about him. He was so different from the other leader. He had been brought in to replace another team leader who was enormously liked and admired by the team. This man was not fun or smart like the one he replaced and he had been imposed on the group.
>
> I kept looking for something about him that I could genuinely like. He was driving me to the airport after one of the sessions, and I don't know what possessed me to ask the question, but I intuitively asked him if he had an alcohol problem. I don't know where that came from, but he started to talk about it and he admitted that he was an alcoholic. Once he acknowledged the alcohol problem, my relationship with him shifted, and I was able to work with him.
>
> *Barbara Bunker*

Dimension 5: Risk: Willingness to Lance the Wound

The most alive questions carry an element of *risk.* We are asking something that invites in the unknown, and there is no guarantee what the outcome will be. Taking a risk requires that we trust ourselves and be willing to make a mistake. This directly links to the state of our Personal Foundations of Integrity, Acceptance, and Courage. If these Personal Foundations are strong, we are willing to take risks while developing questions. Taking a risk can ignite our creativity and sense of contribution. Avoiding risk can result in a superficial intervention.

The best questions might be uncomfortable, and we may fail to pose these critical questions out of habit, fear, blind spots, or assumptions. When the asker is actually seeking, open to the unknown, the questions become remarkably revealing. Each question becomes a step along the path of creativity.

Exercise

Think for a moment about a challenging work situation that involves high risk for you. It might be behaviors, leadership decisions, or opening up/naming secrets.

1. Describe how naming this would require *courage* on your part. What part of you is being challenged? Where is the fear? Why would you even do such a crazy thing?

2. What would you be summoning up within yourself to be able to commit to taking a course of action?

The process of developing a deep, probing, "risk-taking" question requires this same kind of courage, trust, and commitment. The question may be one that has never been asked. The question may trigger issues of personal risk for the consultant, such as, "Is this the question that will get me fired?" The question may challenge all of our expectations and presumptions about the client and the situation.

Following are some questions to explore around risk:

- What is at stake for me personally in asking this question?
- What is the risk for me if I do not ask this question?
- What might I discover if I ask this question?
- What might I miss if I failed to ask this question?
- What is the risk to the client if I ask this question?
- What is the risk to the client if I do not ask this question?

Dimension 6: Timing: Now Is the Only Time There Is

If asking a particular question is worth the risk, is the *timing* right for the question? There are four aspects to awareness of timing:

1. The consultant's connection with what is happening *now.*
2. The timing of the person receiving the question.
3. The impact of the question itself.
4. The relationship of individual timing to group process.

At the heart of timing is a focus on what is happening *here* and *now.* This begins with an attunement to our own inner situation in present time. We might ask ourselves the following questions:

- What is happening with me right now?
- What is my frame of mind right now?
- How grounded am I right now?
- How distracted am I right now?
- What "head talk" is taking place in me right now?

To stay present in the here and now requires a great deal of concentration and applied awareness. A simple question loop can be used to keep our attention focused on the present, so that we can train ourselves to be observant while developing conscious questions:

- What is happening *now?*
- What *just* happened?
- What is happening *now?*
- What is happening *next?*
- What is happening *now?*

(Repeat)

Why is it important to focus on the *now?* When we start on a trip, we look at a map and ask the first question: "Where are we now?" Then we look at where we want to go. As we travel, we check the map again and again for where we are now, where we are going, and where we have been. It is the cycle of the journey. (Of course, if there are children present, their focus is simply, "Are we there yet?")

It is the focus on what is happening *now* that expands the consciousness of the question. Think about a trip on which a map was not used. Perhaps it was a plane trip. You might have boarded the plane, found your aisle seat, and focused on a good book. This may have been the extent of the trip until you arrived, with a few diversions around food and the restroom. But the focus was not on "Where are we now? What are we flying over at this time?"

If we are going to be more than passengers passively transported from one place to another, we need to pay attention to the present, as well as the past and the future, and to make skillful use of maps to help orient the now to other times.

The second aspect of awareness of timing is *the timing of the person receiving the question.* The major impact of a well-timed question is on the client. Inclusion of the client, the client's place in the process, and the client's own timing is essential. Then we can focus on where the question is leading in the change process.

Each person is unique, with a change process that is unique to that person as well. Inclusion of clients will mean that we are including the four keys of their "state of being"—their level of acceptance, seeking, courage, and curiosity. Inclusion of clients' timing involves awareness of their state of being in the present moment.

When we are focused on the client's individual timing, we naturally generate "I wonder" questions:

- I wonder what is going on with the client right now?

- I wonder what he or she is *thinking* about the questions and the answers that are coming up?

- I wonder what he or she is *feeling* about the questions and the answers that are coming up?

When this kind of interest is present in the one *asking* the questions, the one *responding* to the questions is present as well. The client becomes included in the question, and in this way the question becomes more conscious.

The client's level of consciousness will affect his or her timing clock. As conscious consultants, we have been cultivating awareness and an appreciation of active change for some time. When we engage clients in a process of change, we have to remember that they do not have the same training or experience that we have in this area, and their interest level may be different as well.

The third aspect of awareness of timing is *the impact of the question itself.* Change occurs step by step, and the only step we can take is the next one. That step will be unique for every moment, every person, and every situation. People build a new way of operating in a sequential manner. All too often this simple truth is overlooked. People can be so impatient to arrive at the destination that they neglect to build the road they need to get there. Being sensitive to the impact of the question will help us to determine when the time is right for a particular question, enabling the change process to move forward in the right sequence and at the right pace.

> I seek to know what is true for me right now and what makes sense for me
> right now. Working around the globe has helped me to understand that the

more different ways I know to approach something the better I am able to work with different cultures.

It helps to have things in the toolkit, but we need to be flexible with what goes in. It is important to understand that there is no right way to do anything; there are just multiple ways. Appreciative Inquiry is a way of being with the foundational question: "How can we be the most appreciative in the moment?" It is not knowing how to do a thing well, but knowing how to be in the moment, being willing to explore what is called for *now*.

Jane Magruder Watkins

The final aspect of timing of the question concerns *the relationship of individual timing to group process*. Whatever individual or group process model is used (Action Research [French & Bell, 1990], Dyer [1977], Schein [1988], Nadler [1977], or Drexler, Sibbet, and Forrester [1988]), groups go through the following stages:

1. *Identification:* Identification with other people is a desire to understand and learn from one another and to establish a relationship. It is a discovery of who we are individually and in relation to each other.

2. *Connection:* We decide that we want to share more fully with one another.

3. *Trust:* We discover how safe we are and how deep we will go with our connection.

4. *Common Ground:* As trust develops, we become aware that there is common ground around similar goals, thoughts, and actions.

5. *Blending:* We learn to use what is different among the members of the group to come up with a new and unique way that moves the group forward. We see that there may be something common, even in perceived differences.

6. *Co-creation:* We look for how we can best relate to one another as partners in establishing this relationship and what we are each doing in the process of this creation.

7. *Acknowledgment:* We acknowledge that we are sharing this experience. To acknowledge does not mean there must be a change in someone's opinion or view; it is simply identifying a shared experience in which consideration of beliefs can take place.

Within each of these stages, there is a different dynamic. Therefore, the questions will be different at each stage. Both the consultant and the client will be in a different state of being during *blending* than they were in *identification.* Each will have new knowledge, and therefore the questions will be different. The meaning of the question will be different at the beginning of the process because the shared assumptions have not been developed; this will shift as the team has shared experiences. It is possible that the consultant will be asking the intuitive questions at the beginning of the process and then, toward the end, the client members will be asking the intuitive questions.

Dimension 7: The Problem: Will the Real Problem Please Stand Out?

Symptoms are not the problem; they are caused by a problem. It is all too easy for consultants to ask questions that seek solutions for symptoms without first having discovered the problem. This approach is just a short-term fix. Before we are ready to ask "What is the solution?" we need to learn how everything is working and whether improvements are necessary or even possible.

As consultants, we are often called in to execute an intervention that our client sees as the solution to a problem. The client may or may not be correct in his or her assessment. To fully serve the client, we need to discover enough about what is actually happening to enable us to make our own diagnosis of the problem. We need to describe the symptoms present in the situation without assuming that the symptoms are the actual problem. The accurate description of a problem is absolutely necessary to achieve an appropriate solution. We can then work out a tailor-made intervention that will address the real problem. Boiling symptoms down to core problems allows us to do work that is lasting and strong.

Consider the example of "Marlo," who says that her problem is that she is not making enough money. While not having enough income certainly creates problems, is it the core problem? Or is it a symptom of a problem? Perhaps Marlo wildly overspends and, no matter what her income, she will never have enough money. In this case, finding ways to increase income would not solve Marlo's problem, since the real problem has not been addressed.

Another example would be "Brandon," who decides, "I am lonely. The problem is that I don't have a partner in my life." The actual problem is being lonely. One of the possible solutions is to build a close relationship. But there might be other solutions, and Brandon's solution might not solve the real problem, because people can feel lonely even within a relationship.

Following are some questions that might help us discover the real problem:

- What doubts do I have about my own performance, skill, capability, or expertise?
- How accurate are these doubts?
- Do I set up myself up for failure?
- If I am uncomfortable, what is the source of my discomfort?
- Is it possible that I lie to myself about the source of my discomfort? If I removed the supposed source of discomfort, would I then be comfortable?
- How long has this discomfort been a "symptom"?
- Does the symptom seem to have a pattern?
- Is it possible to still have the symptom after the proposed solution is achieved?

Questions about the nature of the real problem will help us to see what we are dealing with.

> I was at a board meeting, and the president of the organization was talking about the new directions he saw the board taking, how these changes would affect the governance structure, and so on. He asked for discussion and how the board members felt about what he had suggested. No one said anything.
>
> I thought I felt a current or an upset in the room. I was feeling something, but I was not sure this was the place to bring up what I was feeling. The president kept talking to fill the void and kept asking whether anyone wanted to talk about his suggestions. Each time no one had anything to say, I would say to myself, "There is something going on in the room. We don't seem to be willing to deal with the real problem."
>
> The president finally said, "This is the last time!" So I summoned my courage and said, "I'm not sure what is going on, but for me this change represents failure on my part as a board member. I wonder whether the changes would be necessary if I were doing my job."
>
> There was a great deal of conversation that followed about the direction we should be going. Meetings later, I was asked to serve as vice president that year and president the next year because I was seen as someone who was willing to put the question on the table. In the past, I have faced issues about how to "show up in a way that really makes a difference." I have learned that

this means not just leaving a message, but having the courage to say it out loud that makes a difference.

Jim Earley

The organization was looking at a solution to a problem that was not really the problem. At the same time as the president was discussing the issue, Jim was running a parallel internal conversation about doubting his intuitive feelings about what else was going on in the room, wondering how accurate his feelings were, looking at his own discomfort with the discussion and his own feelings. In the past, he may not have said anything and there would not have been an impact. But with this incident, he chose to say something out loud and it had a huge impact. He helped the group to see what was going on by asking his internal question out loud. And at the same time, he was able to help himself to see that he sometimes had doubts about his own abilities. When he "showed up," he was able to make a difference.

Reflective Questions

This chapter has been about cultivating the art of asking questions by recognizing that the questions come first of all from deep within ourselves as consultants. Who we are, what we know, and how conscious we are determine both the questions and their impact. A question is based on where we stand with our Personal Foundations. Asking the question sets the change process in motion.

Throughout this chapter, answers have not been addressed except as the product of a good question. Answers in themselves neither create nor lead to action. Answers do nothing until they are used. That is when the change occurs. Answers may lead to other questions, but it is the asking of the question that brings about an action.

The following questions and reflective comments are intended as a "starter list" that can be used to help inspire your own conscious questions. Feel free to create your own categories, add favorite questions, and in general expand this list as you continue to expand yourself. A useful technique is to create handouts of some of these questions to share with your clients to start a dialogue.

Questions That Open Doors for Me

- What would I do if I had no limits?
- What is the meaning of this event or experience in my life?
- If I were transparent, what would people say about me?

- How would I describe myself?
- How would others describe me?
- In what ways was I truthful today?
- What did I notice today that I have not noticed for a while?
- Today, did I behave in a way that made me proud?
- How much am I willing to be seen?
- How much space do I let the client have for his or her truth?
- Why do I do what I do?
- What are my work values?
- If I were to ask myself a question about my personal values, what would it be?
- How would I know whether my structure is supporting my intentions, desires, and needs?
- What would be clues that there are wobbly parts in my foundations?
- How would I discover the meaning and impact of my agreements with myself about my work?
- How do I know how my personal growth has helped in my personal life?
- How do I know how my personal growth has helped me with my career?
- How do I know my personal growth has helped with my client results?
- How do I say "no" to anything I feel I am not ready for or that violates my values?
- How do I determine and honor my own priorities?
- If I am functioning better, how do I know that?
- How can I do progress checks on my own change program?
- How does self-respect equate to success for me?
- When I change, how can I discover how much I have changed?

Questions That Open Doors for Others

- What would happen if . . . ?
- What are the possibilities?

- What do you need to know at this time?
- How can you find out what the real problem is?
- If you could choose anything, what would you want?
- How can you make a difference?
- What values are you comfortable with?
- What values in your organization do you struggle with?
- What did you learn today?
- What is an important event in your life and why?
- What do you want to be known for?

Questions That Connect Clients with Their Work

- What is unique about your work?
- What kinds of decisions do you make, or are going to make?
- What in the past influenced your decisions?
- What in the present influences your decisions?
- What is developing that causes you concern?
- What is developing that causes you hope?
- What is your belief system about your obligations to your work?
- If you could construct the perfect company culture for this organization, what would it be like?

Questions That Cause Learning

- What surprised me today?
- How do my insights shift what I know?
- Why did I do the best I could today?
- What situations was I able to accept today and how did I do this?
- What insights did I have today?
- To what have I committed my life?

- What did I say "no" to today?
- In what ways was I congruent with my identity today?

Questions About My Relationship with the Client

- How have I been strengthened personally by each client relationship?
- What are my expectations of my work with clients? Are these expectations reasonable?
- In what ways am I authentic with my clients?
- How do I choose the work I will do with my clients?
- What do I deserve as a result of doing work with a client?
- What do I value most about the work that I do?
- What do I give up in order to be successful?
- What are the barriers to my success?
- How have I grown as a result of doing my work?
- What are my standards for success?
- How do I ensure that my work is successful?
- How was I interested in and curious about the client?
- Was I interested in making money or looking good?
- How can I learn more about the problem?
- Did I view the client in terms of "right" or "wrong"?
- In what ways was I listening deeply?
- What happened when I trusted my intuition?
- In what new ways was I paying attention to others?
- In what ways did I help the client to reconnect with what they already knew?
- In what ways did I connect in a personal and open way?
- What do I say to myself about the work that I do?
- What do I say to others about the work that I do?
- What do I usually tell myself about why I am doing this work?

- If I listened to the deep voices within me, what would I become aware of as reasons for doing the work I do?

- What does the work actually bring to me?

- What do I imagine that it brings to others?

- What questions do I need to ask myself about the client while I am working with him or her?

- In what state do I need to be to ask provocative questions?

- How is my body reacting now to the client and the information the client has given me?

- What do I sense that the client is projecting on me? Can I handle it?

- What do I need the client to know about me to proceed?

- What do I need to know about the client to proceed?

- What seems to happen with *every* client? What do I always seem to encounter?

- Some things happen no matter what I do. How do I react to them?

- How do I handle my surprise?

- Will this work be fun?

- Will I be a success doing this project?

- How has my awareness of my foundations been clarified with each interaction with my clients? Can I fill in more of my foundational picture?

- How has my structure strengthened the relationship with each of my clients?

Questions to Ask Myself About the Client

- What is the client's perception of change?

- How do I get a sense of the client's reality? What are the clues?

- How do I find out what the client's agenda is?

- How do I find out what is going on in the organization?

- What is broken that the client doesn't want to fix?

- Where is the resistance?

- Who wants a change and why?

- What is the client ready for next?

Developing Your Own Questions

In this chapter, we have outlined seven dimensions for the conscious question. We've provided many sample questions in the previous section and, at the beginning of this chapter, some powerful questions that Alexandra Merrill asks herself about her political and spiritual identity were listed.

For each of the dimensions listed below, first describe yourself as the dimension applies to you. Develop a few of your own questions that help you to identify how to integrate this dimension into your question asking. You might also wish to develop a separate sheet for how this dimension applies to an individual client.

1. *State of Being:* The Seeker on a Quest

2. *Knowledge:* What We Know or Do Not Know

3. *Insight:* What Does the Question Really Mean?

4. *Intuition:* Now Where Did That Come From?

5. *Risk:* The Willingness to Lance the Wound

6. *Timing:* Now Is the Only Time There Is

7. *The Problem:* Will the Real Problem Please Stand Out

(5)

Setting Up Agreements with Myself and with My Clients

Actions Contain Agreements

Throughout this book we have been looking at the deep structure of active change—in particular, bringing to light factors that may not be apparent but that have a strong influence on how change will proceed. It is the authors' position that active change involves bringing this deep structure into conscious awareness. In this chapter we explore an underlying dimension of the *Act* stage of the Active Change Model—creating *agreements* that support healthy change in ourselves and in our clients.

An act is when something moves from a state of possibility to a state of reality. It takes energy to convert potentiality to actuality, and this may appear as a behavior, process, or stage of a process. An action can take place in a split second, engaging a process of change. For example, I hear a loud crashing noise downstairs in the basement, jump, and begin moving toward the sound to see what has just broken.

Each moment of action contains within it an enormous amount of information that, brought into awareness, can be helpful. Every action contains *agreements* with ourselves and with others. These agreements can be either conscious or unconscious, which will strongly affect whether the change that takes place is active or reactive. Conscious agreements prepare the way for active change. (See Figure 5.1.)

In this chapter, we will look at three kinds of agreements:

- Conscious agreements with ourselves about our foundation development.
- Conscious agreements with ourselves about our professional work.
- Conscious agreements with our clients.

Figure 5.1. How Agreements Relate to the Foundations

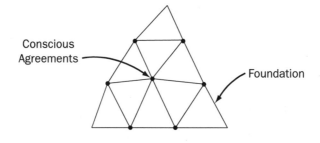

Note: In this section of the geodesic sphere the lines represent our foundations, while the connections between the lines represent our agreements. Our agreements are what gives form and structure to our foundations. If our agreements are conscious, these links are intentionally created and strengthened.

Conscious Agreements with Ourselves About Our Foundation Development

One way we can describe ourselves is in terms of the current condition of our Personal Foundations. Because we are complex creatures, their present condition will be based on our values, beliefs, attitudes, and the meanings that we put on ideas, objects, events, and principles as we experience them through sensations, feelings, and thoughts. From birth, our situations are always undergoing change, some conscious and some unconscious.

Imagine that there is an attic in your house. In the attic is your grandmother's rocking chair, a trunk full of artifacts from your great-grandparents, your mother's tricycle, your father's bicycle, your brother's baseball mitt, and your own trunk filled with scrapbooks, photos, special mementos, and so on. Some of these items have stories that go with them, such as "I walked five miles through the snow to get to school" and "Your great-grandparents came to the United States on a boat, making hard sacrifices along the way." We can "translate" the items in the attic into stories with meaning for us—grandmother's behaviors, great-grandparents' actions, the things that mother, father, or brother did "to you" as a child.

You may have thought of the attic contents as things that belong to others that are just being stored in your attic. But because you have left all this "stuff" in your attic for so long, you now have an agreement, perhaps unconscious, that it is *your* stuff.

In the same way, whether we are aware of it or not, we have made agreements about which parts of our upbringings we accept as parts of ourselves. Growing up, we may have decided to keep our family values of working hard, telling the truth, and being kind. We have formed an agreement with ourselves around these values. This agreement will be repeatedly tested by situations in which we could lie or be unkind. It is like a poke from the universe to see whether we meant what we said. With each situation, we are faced with the choice of keeping our agreements with ourselves or breaking them.

On the other hand, there may be parts of ourselves that we have received from our family history that we wish to change. We decide what is in the attic that does not serve us—we decide who we want to be—and we make a conscious choice to be different.

> My father had been a physical and emotional bully toward my mother and
> their seven children. I was the oldest son, wanting to be like my father, but

also wanting deeply to prove to my mother than I was different from (and better than) my father. I never found a way of standing up to my father or of protecting my mother and brothers and sisters (the job of a big brother, I believed) from him.

After a number of years working as a consultant, I suddenly became aware, with the help of much personal development and therapy, that I was building a professional reputation and career out of searching for, finding, and then developing effective relationships with bully-type autocrats. Moreover, my consulting interventions were designed to help employees (that is, my brothers and sisters) challenge their autocratic bosses. What a shock it was for me to realize that I had been using client organizations and the autocrats within them to achieve what I had been unable to achieve with my family.

Phil Mix

It took some personal work on his part, but Phil was able to see a link between what was in his attic and what was appearing with his clients. Seeing this made it possible for him to make a conscious agreement to be different—to make a new agreement.

An important part of agreements has to do with the establishment of boundaries. Earlier in the book, Geoff Bellman spoke about the dynamics between "yes" and "no" in relationship to boundaries. Healthy boundaries help to ensure that neither party will be mistreated in the relationship, which means that we have to include ourselves as well as our clients.

An example of how this dynamic between "yes" and "no" plays out with someone whose agreements do not include both himself and others comes from "Daniel," who entered the field of OD through T-group and encounter-group experiences. During that period, he experienced blunt and direct feedback. He describes his seven-, ten-, and twenty-one-day experiences as "brutal." He has formed a belief that, because he grew a lot from that form of feedback, others would benefit from the same approach.

During his work with clients, Daniel would ask his clients if they wanted him to give them feedback. When they responded "yes" to that question, he would give feedback that was sometimes so blunt and direct that it was hurtful. Every once in a while, one of Daniel's clients would tell him, "That hurt." Instead of stopping to hear what the client had said, Daniel would discount the person by saying that he was modeling his own early experiences with feedback. The client

*had been dismissed because he or she tried to give blunt feedback. Daniel has a
different set of agreements for himself than for his clients.*

Knowing what is in our attic—beliefs, thoughts, feelings, experiences, and so
forth—helps us to understand how we define ourselves, and the boundaries we
agree on to delineate the relationship between ourselves and other people.

> Early in my career, my boundaries were permeable. I was so eager to figure
> out what others wanted that I did not have a good clear sense of myself. Char-
> lie Seashore refers to our fear of the "core of rot," which is that bundle of inse-
> curities inside of us that we don't want to deal with. Most consultants have
> done emotional homework, taking themselves on and looking at their own
> interior life. This cannot be done alone easily. Generally, there is not much that
> I am shocked by because I have looked at the stuff within myself. Being able
> to accept others' quirks has been easy because I accept that part of myself.
>
> *Barbara Bunker*

Agreements also have an important connection to goals. When we set goals, we
are making agreements with ourselves about what we want to do in the future—
and probably how we want to do them as well. For example, if one of our goals is
to achieve better physical health, we may decide to avoid sugar for the coming year
in order to accomplish that goal. This is an agreement with ourselves about how
we will act. We can expect that the agreement will be tested, as when we go out for
dinner and the waiter says, "How about some dessert tonight?" We will have many
opportunities to stick to the agreement or, if it is not working, to renegotiate it.

Making agreements with ourselves gives force to the desire to act. We can have
a vague wish to act differently than in the past but find that we continue to take the
same actions. Or we can make a clear and conscious agreement with ourselves to
clean something that no longer serves us out of the attic and thereby move closer
to a desired stage.

> Over the years, I have finally heard my calling. I am in the authenticity busi-
> ness. I help people, professionals, or organizations identify, quicken, and support
> the search for what is true and real. Once discerned, I encourage courage to act
> on the insights and wisdom to make adept choices as leaders. For me, leadership
> is serving the promise of authenticity inside the actor and outside in the world.
>
> Although I do not remember where or how the idea came to me, I devel-
> oped a concept that has helped many people and organizations take charge

of their own lives. I call it the "Exit Card." I not only advocate it; I use it myself. Every time I take on a consulting/leadership education contract, I fill out the exit card for myself. It consists of two parts:

If I do not take this job, I could be doing. . . .
Under the following three conditions, I will use my card and not take the job:

1.

2.

3.

Understanding myself and being clear about my exit card helps me ask tough questions, confront tough situations, and assist organizations and people to address deep value issues triggered by the voice of authenticity and the necessity of courage.

I recommend that internal consultants do the same. If they feel and believe that they are trapped and will not leave, they will remain as co-conspirators and support the organization going where it should not go. Anyone desperate for a job colludes with the bosses and erodes and undermines authenticity. The organization will live the lie and self-destruct in the long term.

Bob Terry

Conscious Agreements with Ourselves About Our Professional Work

Many people who choose careers as change agents have similar reasons: We like to help others, we feel we have something to offer, and we find being involved in change exciting and creative. We also want to have an impact. *Why* we choose this career may form a basis for our agreements with ourselves about *how* we want to do our work. When these agreements are created consciously and deliberately, they can give powerful support to our professional lives; otherwise, they can sneak up and bite us.

Exercise

Ask yourself the following questions to clarify and reflect on your agreements with yourself about your work:

1. What do you want to experience as a result of your work with clients?

2. What do you actually experience?

3. What are the strengths that you bring to your work?

4. What is the gap between what you hope to get and what you really get with the work you do?

5. What are your formerly unconscious and now conscious agreements with yourself?

6. What are the new agreements you are making with yourself?

7. What steps can you include in your Foundation Development Plan to ensure that you are changing?

"Fred" is an external consultant who consciously practiced the Active Change Model and worked with the seven questions above. His story illustrates how the questions can be effectively applied to professional development.

Fred reported, "I feel that I'm doing good work with my clients, but for some reason my practice isn't growing the way I think it should. Most of my contracts involve working with teams in medium-sized companies. I've helped them improve their process and efficiency. I feel that there's more that I could do for them, but I'm not sure how to go deeper. What's more, I'm noticing that my clients are not calling me for the bigger jobs."

Using the Active Change Model, Fred's first step along his personal change process was to perceive and describe what he was noticing with his clients. He exercised considerable courage to do this, letting go of a lot of ego simply to accept that this was the truth. This is what Fred learned from considering these questions:

1. *What do you want to experience as a result of your work with clients?*

   "I hope the team members will be able to develop a strong personal working relationship with each other as well as work on technical improvements.

   "I would like to help the team members learn to have healthy relationships and resolve conflict.

   "I want to have the client respect me as a competent professional.

   "I want to know that the clients' experience was so good that they refer me to other potential clients."

2. *What do you actually experience?*

> *"At the beginning of my work, I feel anxious and concerned about whether or not I have the right design or whether the client will find me to be an experienced and knowledgeable consultant.*

> *"I am concerned that my skills and abilities may not be strong enough to pull the team through, especially when team conflicts begin to emerge.*

> *"Every time the team members show tension, withdraw, are silent, or sit with their arms tightly folded across their chests, I am anxious about my ability to help them.*

> *"Because of my own anxiety around conflict, I hurry the team to finish the process work, rather than addressing the causes of the tension.*

> *"When I begin to hurry the team, I become more dominant in my facilitation, offering solutions, charging forward over people, and ignoring the body language."*

3. *What are the strengths that you bring to your work?*

> *"I enjoy people and I enjoy working with them.*

> *"I really care about the success of the people I work with.*

> *"I know I am good at the technical parts of process design work.*

> *"I work very hard to ensure that my clients have a good experience."*

4. *What is the gap between what you hope to get and what you really get with the work you do?*

> *"I feel there is a lot left unsaid during my work with the teams.*

> *"I question my ability to handle conflict. I have always avoided conflict or tried to handle it quickly. I generally don't spend time seeking to understand what the other person is saying or how that relates to what I am saying. In other words, I panic.*

> *"I often feel that when others are in conflict, it's somehow my fault. I try to distract them and resolve the issues quickly without knowing whether I really am resolving anything. I just want peace for now.*

> *"I am always in a marketing mode because I am not called back after one or two projects."*

During this exploration, Fred began to realize where his pattern came from. He had a belief that there should always be a winner and a loser. He did not want to be a "loser," so he would find ways to avoid conflict. By avoiding conflict, he found that he was always "giving in" or "giving up" in order to have the conflict go away. Through the process of looking at his wants, experience, strengths, and gaps, he became aware of unconscious agreements that he had made.

5. *What are your formerly unconscious and now conscious agreements with yourself?*

> *"I cannot be authentic with my clients because it is risky.*
>
> *"I will doubt my capabilities with my clients.*
>
> *"I will avoid conflict or handle it quickly no matter what.*
>
> *"I will work very hard for my clients to compensate for my fears about conflict.*
>
> *"I am not worthy of self-respect."*

With this discovery, Fred acknowledged that his agreements ensured that he would always "lose." So he decided to redo his agreements.

6. *What are the new agreements you are making with yourself?*

> *"I will state what I am feeling when I am feeling it, because that will help me to be more aware of how I am dealing with conflict.*
>
> *"I will learn to look at conflict as a way of learning how everyone, including myself, is perceiving an issue.*
>
> *"I understand that for a relationship to go deeper, there needs to be an exchange of views. This may mean there is conflict. I will choose to see that as a way to form a deeper relationship between others and myself—a passageway to something better."*

Fred then took his conscious agreements and identified some actions that would help him learn how to become more congruent with his new agreements.

7. *What steps can you include in your Foundation Development Plan to ensure that you are changing?*

> *"Learn to practice appropriate silence during client conflict, allowing them to experience their own tension, and learn to find ways to resolve it themselves.*

"Ask the clients during the contracting phase how they usually manage conflict and what they want help with.

"Remind myself that I have a deep desire to help the team members learn how to have healthy relationships and resolve conflict, and remain aware that the conflict is not directed at me.

"Remember my skills for listening and reflecting back to my clients, and plan to develop these talents more completely.

"Get some training for myself in order to develop more tools and experience so I can separate emotionally from conflicts that I am not a party to.

"Plan to take a 'time out' when involved in my own personal conflict so I can find other ways to deal with it outside of my usual pattern. I will do this by referring to my 'time-out list,' which will include the things that I learned in my training."

Fred followed the Active Change Model to discover his unconscious agreements by tracing the symptoms back far enough so that what was behind the symptoms became more conscious. From there he was able to reformulate his agreements into conscious ones. The result was that he felt stronger as a consultant, his work became stronger, and his practice began to shift into obtaining longer-term projects and more referrals to other clients.

Exercise

This exercise is to further clarify aspects of yourself that might be mostly unconscious but that are making a strong impact on your professional life. Read through the list of questions below and see which ones seem sensitive to your personal development work in relationship to your professional work. Pick three to five questions to explore further.

1. What do you value most about the work that you do?

2. What are your beliefs about money and worth?

3. What are your success criteria?

4. What do you fear about success?

5. What are your barriers to success?

6. What is your definition of security?

7. How much does that definition drive the kind of work you seek?

8. How does your work stretch you?

9. How does your work inhibit you?

10. What are your personal doubts about your own performance, skills, capability, and expertise?

11. How do your doubts manifest themselves in your work?

12. If your client experiences failure, do you consider it your failure as well?

13. Is it possible that you unconsciously sabotage your clients' process?

14. What did you learn about work from your parents?

15. What did you learn about success from your parents?

16. How do you describe abundance?

17. What do you give up in order to be successful?

18. How much effort do you put into controlling work outcomes?

19. Do you commit to things that you cannot control?

20. How much of your drive for impact is to help *others* change?

21. How have you impacted others when you have changed?

22. What is really important to you?

23. In what ways is self-respect important for you?

24. What are your values around giving?

25. What happens to you when others give to you?

26. What would make you feel dependent on your work?

27. What would make you feel independent of your work?

28. How would you describe your full potential to others?

29. What do you do to recover when you are not successful?

30. When you change, how do you discover how much you have changed?

31. In what ways do you want to be happy with your work and with yourself?

32. What would you list in a "grateful" book about your success?

33. How do you celebrate a job well done?

Write down your answer to each of the questions you have selected from the list. Then write down the agreements you have with yourself in this area—first the "old" agreement that you have been operating under, then, if there is one, the "new" agreement that you would like to replace it with. Following is an example prepared by "Genevieve":

Question 5. What Are Your Barriers to Success?

They seem to be self-barriers. I seem to get close to success and then pull back because I am afraid of what will happen when I really am successful. I get a lot of awards and kudos for things that I have done, and I seem to forget about them as soon as I get them. It is like spending a lot of time shopping for a new suit and then dropping it in the garbage can as I come into the house.

Old Agreement: *When success is close, start on a new project so there is always a new achievement on the horizon.*

New Agreement: *I will stop and have a mini-party for myself—some way of celebrating an accomplishment—and I will relish the moment of something coming to a finish for me.*

Question 14. What Did You Learn About Work from Your Parents?

My parents were farmers in Idaho. They worked physically hard from dawn to dusk. There was a certain amount of pride in going into town to do shopping with dirty fingernails. It was a nonverbal statement that they had been working hard. What I learned was that I needed to work "hard" in order to achieve anything. This means that I need to do a project faster and better than anyone else, do more projects at the same time, and excel at all of them.

Old Agreement: *I have to expend superhuman effort in order to be recognized.*

New Agreement: *I will define what is "good work" as I start to work with each client, and that will be my own internal standard that I am happy with.*

Question 18. How Much Effort Do You Put into Controlling Work Outcomes?

I put a lot of effort into controlling the outcomes, and this seems to come from childhood when I could not control what was going on in my family. The family system was chaotic, uncertain, and unsafe. I don't want to experience that at work, and I will do anything to ensure that it is not chaotic, uncertain, and unsafe.

Old Agreement: *I will search out all of the details and plan for them so there will be no surprises.*

New Agreements: *I will take a baby step first. I will not search for all of the answers, let what happens happen, and see whether I can learn from that— see it as a positive and take joy in experiencing the unknown.*

This exercise should help us to develop an understanding of how important it is to expose our unconscious agreements in order to have healthier consulting practices. It will help us become more aware of the boundaries we are setting in the kind of work we will do.

I have said "no" to work that I would love to do. Twenty years ago, Sheila and I consciously decided how the work we do could serve our lives, both individually and as a family. So we decided that I would not work more than 100 days a year for money. I have stuck to that agreement all but one year. Most of my years I have averaged about 75 days. We revisit this agreement all the time. Right now, I consult for pay from one to eight days a year. The rest of my time is given to my family and my community, helping this world become a better place to live. That is a boundary that we established and have honored for the most part, and it has served me well in terms of enriching my life.

In my work, I say "no" to some work based on principle. For example, I will not work in the tobacco industry. Some work I will decline because I am uncomfortable with it, such as working in the cosmetics industry. Other work I decline because it is not good for me. For example, I will work with executives in the health care industry but will not take on a change process because I don't like what I do with myself when I am working there. I feel like I take on the illness of the system. The client may find my work satisfactory-to-successful, but there is a big impact on me—I don't like how I feel when I am there.

Geoff Bellman

In reaching these strong positions about client work, Geoff has pulled up deep parts of himself with great clarity and has given them power by formulating agreements with himself about the kind of work he will do.

For some of us, an internal dialogue is not enough—we need to include external input from friends and family.

As I age, I wish to work with clients closer to home and I've been reflecting on how I want to "select" or "accept" my new clients.

As an extrovert, my decisions about new directions tend to be worked out in stimulating and sometimes discomforting conversations with friends and colleagues. A few of these friends and colleagues have expressed some curiosity, a few more feel judgment directed at them by my even raising the questions, and others listen politely, perhaps because they've already resolved the client choice questions for themselves or because they have no interest.

Over time, I've heard colleagues express numerous ways to make these choices, some expressing a single choice criterion, others several. I've discovered it takes effort to make conscious and sort out our fundamental values and motives.

Ken Shepard

Ken collected from his conversations with colleagues a list of alternative and possibly conflicting values around the agreements we make in determining the kinds of clients we wish to work with. He then formulated his ideas as "I choose" statements and created the following exercise for others to evaluate their own choices.

Exercise*

Read through the value choices slowly and reflect on how true each of the values statements below may be for you on a scale from 1 to 10 (1 = not at all true; 10 = true to a great extent). Next, rank order the statements by importance, with the most important motivating choice first. And for a final clarification, refine the wording to fit your values and re-rank if necessary.

____ "I choose clients as close to home as possible. I love my family and want to support them as best I can with minimum time away and without the exhaustion and jet lag of long trips."

____ "I choose clients who pay the highest consulting rates. It's ironic that some of these companies have the greatest corporate responsibility issues, but maybe I can help from the inside. I need a high income,

---

both to meet my own financial goals and to provide for others at a standard I choose."

_____ "I choose clients in the [fill in] sector. I got my experience there, know lots of potential clients, and although I'm aware many of them are not good corporate citizens, it's not practical to be so picky."

_____ "I choose to work for almost anybody who calls and wants me to work within the law. The market for management consultants is very competitive. I don't have enough work, and I need to pay the mortgage. I'll work for any organization that operates within the laws of the land (employment, environmental, health and safety, et cetera) and doesn't ask me personally to break the law."

_____ "I choose to assist whomever asks for my services regardless of their mission and values or likelihood of producing any results. A 'good' doctor is expected to treat whoever presents themselves at the door. Who am I to judge? Most agree that even the worst criminals deserve good lawyers."

_____ "I choose to help organizations only after I have thought through the kind of good society that I personally want for myself and my family. And then I will work only for those organizations whom I discern most likely to contribute to my personal vision of that good society."

_____ "I choose to work for those clients who know my values and are willing to hire me knowing that I will live by those values. I show potential clients my written ethics statement or the OD profession ethics statement developed by Bill Gellermann and discuss how my values may affect how the project is carried out."

_____ "I choose to work for clients when I know and like them and believe them to be good people."

_____ "I choose to work primarily for privately-held companies when I can know the owners and trust their character and the beneficence of their intent."

_____ "I choose to help only when I perceive the 'ownership system' functions for societal good. That means I choose to work for nonprofits and community-based organizations. Publicly held, global corporations are bad systems that wipe out the best efforts of good people. They are systems out of control. I do not believe they can be saved from the inside."

_____ "I choose to work for clients at the top of the house. I want to be close to the direction setter and to the implementer. I want to have impact."

_____ "I choose to work for those prestigious organizations that will look good on my client list and help me get more clients like them."

_____ "I choose to work for those client systems where I will learn the most. I am most enthused by challenging work where I'm in new situations, developing new concepts, doing research, and writing up my experiences. I'm really a 'clinician' more than a consultant."

_____ "I choose to work for clients who express respect and appreciation for the work that I do for them. I need to be valued. They are warm and inclusive and pay quickly."

Exercise

Now spend some time answering the seven questions provided earlier (repeated below) that will help you clarify and reflect on agreements you have with yourself about your work.

1. What do you want to experience as a result of the work with the client?

2. What do you actually experience?

3. What are the strengths that you bring to your work?

4. What is the gap between what you hope to get and what you really get with the work you do?

5. What are your formerly unconscious and now conscious agreements with yourself?

6. What are the new agreements you are making with yourself?

7. What steps can you include in your Foundation Development Plan to ensure that you are changing?

From the examples provided by Bob Terry with his exit card, Geoff Bellman with his agreements about how much and the kind of work he will do, and Ken Shepard's list of choice values, write your own agreements about the work you do. You may wish to write your agreements using the format on the next page.

Consultant's Sample Self-Agreements

I will . . .

1. Choose the work that I will do with my clients.

2. Choose work so that I won't be driven by simple survival needs.

3. Discover and know who I am through my interactions with others.

4. Identify and follow my own values.

5. Say "no" to anything I feel I am not ready for or that violates my values.

6. Treat others with dignity and respect, so I can receive the same.

7. Determine and honor my own priorities.

8. Not be responsible for others' behaviors, actions, feelings, or problems.

9. Make mistakes and not have to be perfect.

10. Expect honesty from myself.

11. Experience my own feelings.

12. Change my mind based on new information.

13. Be joyful in my interactions with others.

14. Respect my own personal space and time needs.

15. Change and grow at a pace I choose.

16. Decide on my own attitude.

17. Learn about myself from my interactions with others.

18. Treat my physical and emotional health as a priority.

19. Take care of myself.

20. Be uncertain.

When healthy self-agreements are fully integrated into our work, there is a profound shift in our client relationship. As consultants, we offer ourselves as "instruments" of change. We are well-tuned as an instrument when we are clear about the state of our Personal Foundations and have agreements with ourselves about how we function in the world and about the work that we do. We then have appropriate boundaries—with our work product, which reflects the state of our agreements.

Conscious Agreements with Our Clients

Now that we have explored agreements with ourselves, let's look at how we formulate agreements with our clients. The first thing to be clear about is what we are *not* trying to do. Our clients have their own sets of agreements with themselves, just as we do. If we try to control the agreements that clients have with themselves, we are working in an inappropriate way. The sooner we learn this, the sooner we can relax in our work!

When formulating agreements with clients, there are three components that are appropriate and helpful for us to pay attention to:

- The consultant's role in formulating agreements.
- The client's role in formulating agreements.
- The elements of a consultant/client agreement.

The Consultant's Role in Formulating Agreements

As consultants we have a lot of roles, including helper, guide, motivator, and catalyst. It is a particularly important role of ours to help clients define what it is they really want to accomplish with their change efforts. Helping them become clear about expectations and outcomes is also an opportunity to help them discover what they may be doing to help or hinder the change efforts.

When we work with clients, we are working at three levels: individual, team, and organization. Awareness of all three interrelationships is important. On the individual level, we have the opportunity to help clients become more aware of who they are, how they function at work, and how they impact others.

In Chapters 2 and 3, we extensively explored the condition of our Personal Foundations. With increased self-awareness, we have an opportunity to engage in a parallel process with our clients so they can discover the condition of their own Personal Foundations.

One common experience is that people are drawn to their organizations for completion and healing. While this may be a very unconscious process, when it is brought to light many individuals will acknowledge that they are involved in the same kind of personal work that we consultants experience in the work that we have been drawn to. Our clients can discover what is in their "attics" through interactions with their work communities. How they choose to work with the issues relates to the agreements they have for their own self-growth. One of the roles that we can play in individual change is to help our clients see the same kinds of connections that we have discovered in working with the Active Change Model and learn how powerful each of the steps is for increased consciousness.

Once we are helping our clients on an individual level, we can do the deep systemic work of identifying organizational agreements that define the culture, attitudes, and behaviors of the members of the organization. This includes such things as how the organization deals with rumors and secrets, what happens to poor performers, what is rewarded, how dysfunctional team dynamics are addressed, and so on. These are all cultural issues that require organizational *and* individual shifts, many of which begin with self-agreements and agreements about the work individuals do in the work they have chosen.

This brings us back to the question of helping the client find out what he or she really wants to accomplish. Our role is to discover the client's awareness and understanding of the kind of work that is needed and his or her willingness to participate as a partner in the outcome. This understanding ensures that *both* our needs are included in the formulation of the agreement.

> I took on a project in the 1970s and got fired! In retrospect, I learned I should have asked more questions about what the client wanted and expected from me. It was a huge learning. I was hired to do a training unit for managers. I did not ask questions that would get me the right information from the man who hired me. He said that we could try out the material with the participants and then work together to improve it. When I got on stage in front of fifty people, I learned they expected jokes and an entertaining dog-and-pony show. I did not have a slick or funny presentation. It was flat and painful.
>
> When I was through, the client said, "I will call you to see if we will use you for other things." I know what it means when I hear that! It means I am done with this client!
>
> *Barbara Bunker*

We can anticipate that clients will oscillate somewhere between being totally committed and totally resistant during a change process, and that they will not stay in any one place for the whole process. The expectations of clients will shift as they learn more about the dynamics of the change process. Because we, as consultants, have lived and breathed similar processes before, we know what to expect. Clients do not. It is like the difference between riding a roller-coaster for the first time or the fiftieth time! Our role is to anticipate this movement and be clear that we have an agreement to be there for them.

> People are struggling in their jobs, and management wants coaching for them to help them reconcile the 360-degree feedback that is incongruent with how they see themselves. I sense that they are not receptive to hearing it now, and if I say something at this point, they will not only "not hear" the message but will shoot the messenger as well.
>
> I know I can't make someone change, nor do I want to. This may be the wisdom of timing. Some people are direct and confrontational and are able to do something with that. That is not my style. I am a listener and take my cues from what I hear. In the moment, I know whether they are defensive because they are pointing fingers or focusing on external factors, saying things like, "If I had more support . . ." or "If this had not happened. . . ." They are afraid to look at things honestly and accept responsibility.
>
> Trust is the key. It takes patience to avoid "jumping the gun" and to wait until people lower their defenses and are willing to face their issues. Inwardly, they know what they have to work on, but they're afraid to acknowledge this openly. They view this as a loss of control and fear organizational reprisals. When they finally do open up, they experience a new freedom, but they must first believe you have their best interests at heart. This clears the way for "teachable moments." I work on building the relationship so that teachable moments are plentiful. This challenges my core strengths to the fullest extent.
>
> *Ken Hultman*

Besides hitting resistance issues, we can anticipate that clients will test us in order to see whether we are clear about where we stand with our agreements.

> Clients will do a certain kind of testing by making statements such as, "Do you think I should fire him?" It is important not to allow the client to make you the responsible party. With clear boundaries about who I am, I can have clear boundaries with the client and respond by saying something like, "What do you think?" I also find that clients will try to get me to do things for them as a way of pushing the boundaries. I usually respond with a quick "No, absolutely not," and accompany that with a huge smile. This helps to check the impulses that they have to rely on me more during the consulting process.
>
> *Barbara Bunker*

Another role we have as consultants, which is a boundary issue, is to ensure that we are not just taking on an assignment that is beyond our experience level because we are hungry for experience or for money. When we do this, we need to be clear about how we are meeting the needs of the client while we are also focused on our own needs.

Some consultants operate on the idea that they know what the client needs and how the project should be implemented, and they believe their job is to "get the client to change" to what the consultant has deemed best. This approach does not include the client, nor does it honor the client's own wisdom. Including everyone's needs and participation leads to more complete and permanent change.

Here are some tenets that help keep our role in perspective when negotiating agreements with a client:

- Remember whom we are serving at all times.
- Eliminate our personal agendas.
- Let the clients have their own process and do what they need to do.
- Ask enough questions to uncover hidden assumptions.
- Help the clients accurately define their situation.
- Plan for the inevitable messy relationships and conflict.
- Provide education, negotiation, and guidance throughout the project.
- Understand group and individual processes, including timing, choice, and agreement for change.
- Hold clear boundaries and agreements.

If we keep these tenets in front of us, we can be in an open state to discover what the clients want from us as their partners in the change effort. We have found that the following questions help us sort out what is being asked of us during a time when we are establishing agreements with our clients.

1. What outcome does the client want?

2. Is the client clear about what his or her participation will be in the process?

3. How does what the client wants match my agreements with myself about the kind of work I want to do?

4. Is what the client wants actually possible for me to deliver? For anyone else to deliver?

5. Do I agree that what the client wants is helpful to him or her?

6. Is the client able and willing to deliver his or her part?

7. Is what the client wants both realistic and helpful?

8. Do I agree with what the client wants, or am I violating my own agreements if I agree to deliver it?

9. What do I need to negotiate with my client?

10. How do I figure out discrepancies when they appear later?

11. What do I sense that the client is projecting onto me?

12. Can I handle those projections?

13. What do I need the client to know about me to proceed?

14. What do I need to know about the client to proceed?

15. Have we discussed how to maintain clarity throughout the intervention?

16. How will we renegotiate when needed?

Once we have established what the client wants from us, we can enter into a more effective agreement to perform the work.

The Client's Role in Formulating Agreements

The role of the clients during the formation of agreements is simple and straight-forward: To be forthcoming with their expectations about the process and the expected outcomes, and then do what they can to ensure success. Nothing can happen without the clients' participation. If they are willing to share their opinions about process, content, progress, and emotions, they are likely to be more receptive to an active change process.

When I work with clients, I fill out an Exit Card (in my mind). The Exit Card consists of two parts:

If I did not take this job, I could be doing. . . .

Under the following three conditions, I will refuse the job:

1.

2.

3.

When I work with clients, I often have them fill out the card to define their personal and/or professional choices. Some people rename the Exit Card the courage card, the empowerment card, the freedom card, or the choice card. The point is that, without authentic choices, one is trapped and exploitable. With a card, one can stay or leave. One empowers oneself.

This process ensures that we each know who we are in terms of our own identity and opens a door to tell the truth to one another. It helps the clients to face tough personal, professional, and organizational realities and to exhibit the courage to address them in action.

Bob Terry

Bob's exit card provides a foundation for clarity of agreements with his clients. It helps them to establish permission to end the relationship if processes are not effective or if anticipated outcomes are not achieved. It is this very act that helps all parties to see that there is choice about the level of participation during the change process.

As consultants, we have the long list of roles in formulating agreements; the clients have the short list. They have plenty to do just living the change process!

The Elements of a Consultant/Client Agreement

Much has been written from a technical perspective about what to include in client agreements (for example, Block, 2000; Freedman & Zackrison, 2001). Here we are looking more broadly at how we set up the relationship with our clients with clarity based on the work that we have done with Personal Foundations and the Active Change Model.

Four elements are keys to formulating conscious agreements: *Discovery, Inclusion, Success Criteria,* and *Renegotiation.*

Discovery

Discovery is a way of understanding what is really present in terms of client wants, needs, and expectations and seeing whether those fit with our own agreements about wants, needs, and expectations. We make a critical distinction between a "want"—which is nice but not essential to the outcome—and a "need"—which is something necessary, something that we will not be able to do without. Questions help us to discover what is of primary importance to each party.

Inclusion

Inclusion is when the needs (not necessarily the wants) of all parties are supported by the consciousness of respecting boundaries, paying attention to timing, and mutuality of intentions. If we focus on needs rather than on wants, it is usually possible to include everyone.

Success Criteria

As consultants, we strive for a balance between the organization's concerns—meeting financial goals, improving productivity, and addressing stakeholder satisfaction—and the well-being of individuals within the organization. Sometimes consultants have ideas about appropriate goals and success that are different from the clients'. Bringing the consultants' and clients' ideas about success to a more conscious state will help determine whether there is alignment with the kind of work that we wish to do, as well as help the client determine whether we are the right consultant for the job.

When clients are interviewing us, they may be asking themselves, "How can I trust that your work with me will be successful and that my investment of time and money will be worth it?" Our work, of course, will have an impact. It might be positive, negative, or simply a waste of time and resources. Results depend on a great many variables. The consultant can be a powerful catalyst, but does not control the participation of others. What if the movement is halfway to the goal? Is the process then a failure? More broadly, how can we determine cause and effect within a complex organization?

It is likely that our intervention is not the only effort being made for change. How can we determine what results are due to our involvement? Our work as consultants has long been in the realm of undocumented results. We do not have clear measurements for our efforts that relate to the actual work accomplished. Training interventions might include measurement of the number of attendees along with the degree of absorption of the material. However, how do we measure behavioral changes that are linked to productivity or financial results? And a deeper question arises: Do we want to have documented results? This brings us back to our own question about value: "Am I valued, and do I deliver value-added work?"

We can use a process to discover how closely our concept of success matches that of our client. The first step is to discover the client's beliefs about success in his or her organization. Following is a list of questions that you might have the client answer to discover how he or she views success:

Questions to Clarify What Success Means for the Client

1. What in the organization's vision ignites passion and performance?

2. How embedded is "making money" in the organization's mission?

3. What would employees say they value most about the work that they do?

4. What could get in the way of the organization's success?

5. What is the definition of security for the leader of this organization?

6. How does that manifest itself in the decisions that he or she makes?

7. In what ways does this organization sabotage its own success?

8. How do the members of the organization demonstrate entitlement?

9. Where in the organization do members focus on abundance?

10. What is the organization's belief about what needs to be given up, either individually or as a group, in order to be successful?

11. How much control is present in the organization to ensure that there is success?

12. How much empowerment is present in the organization to ensure that there is success?

13. What is the difference between control and empowerment in terms of results?

14. Where does the organization encounter self-imposed limitations around success?

15. In what ways are members of the organization building safety into their success factors?

16. In what ways are the members of the organization investing in their own individual success?

17. In what ways are members of the organization competing for recognition and success? Is that at the expense of other team members? Or in support of other team members?

18. What happens in this organization when a team member is successful?

19. How would the organization describe its growth? Would it include financial, employee, or customer growth?

20. How would members of the organization describe their success with customers?

21. What does the organization use as criteria for progress? What are the measurements?

22. How does the organization celebrate success, both individually and organizationally?

Exercise

In the exercise on page 124, thirty-three questions were presented to help you connect with why you do the work you do. Some of the questions were designed to help you identify your own beliefs about success. Reviewing your answers to those questions and then linking them with the client's answers to the questions above will help you get closer to understanding each other's pictures of success—and therefore closer to a conscious agreement about expectations and outcomes.

This exercise is designed to help you with the comparison process.

1. Take a piece of paper and create three vertical columns. Label the first column "My Success Beliefs." Label the middle column "My Client's Success Beliefs." Label the third column "Matches and Gaps."

2. Go to the list of thirty-four questions on page 124 and use those questions to determine your own beliefs about success. Write these beliefs in column one.

3. Pick a difficult client that you have worked with and write down how you perceive his or her beliefs about success in column two.

4. In the third column identify where you had a match or a gap with that client and how that impacted the success of the work that you did.

Renegotiation

We may have entered our relationship with our clients with what we thought was a shared understanding of what the work could or should be. Both parties had their own pictures, based on their assumptions and the data that was available at the time. Over time, the pictures we each hold become clearer. With that increasing clarity comes the challenge to revisit the agreement that we have with ourselves about the work we do. We remind ourselves and our clients that there is always the opportunity to renegotiate this agreement.

This renegotiation can be of our personal agreements. For example, avoiding sugar may be too difficult, so we renegotiate with ourselves for a "blow out day." We can renegotiate our personal agreements about the work that we will do. We may choose to limit or expand our practice based on our awareness of the condition of our Personal Foundations. And we may wish to have an agreement with our clients that we revisit on a periodic basis how the relationship is working for both of us.

This chapter has focused on various aspects that are at play in agreements we have with ourselves and with clients. Agreements provide the energy and direction for action. They give life, intention, and perspective to our endeavors. Sometimes consultants gloss over agreements in the rush to get to the "real work." However, attention to agreements is a key element in being a conscious consultant and engaging in active change.

On the next page we see how Joan McIntosh has developed her agreements with herself about her work.

Writing Your Own Agreements

Using the sample below as a guide, write out your own agreements about the work that you will do, how you will do it, and what you think the impact will be for you.

A Story About Making and Keeping Agreements with Myself
By Joan McIntosh

In 1996, John and I were on vacation, a time to relax and spend time together. We were talking about my moving from the San Francisco Bay area to the Twin Cities, a decision with significant implications. This decision would impact my relationship with existing clients, based, for the most part, in California. The move would also reallocate the percentages of time I committed to work, relationship, family and friends, community, and self. Since approximately 75 percent of my time was in the "work" slice of the pie, it was the obvious place to start to find an answer to the question.

My Focus Questions

"How can I get more control and more satisfaction in my practice with my clients while continuing to provide the service they expect? What are my criteria for saying 'yes' to work?"

The Answers

- I need to understand what parts of the business I am ready to "sow, grow, harvest, or plow."

- I need to know and be committed to a mix of business, relationships, and the other parts of my life because the business feeds those other parts.

- I need to know where I will get support for the changes I intend to make.

- The solution has to be congruent with my consulting principles (see at end).

- The solution has to be easy to implement.

- The solution has to be grounded in the truth about why I say "yes" or "no" when clients make requests of me.

- The solution needs to be adjusted with experience.

The Results

- My proclivity for always saying "yes" to new work with new or existing clients comes from my childhood, from being rewarded for being "junior mom." Saying "yes" is tied directly to receiving love or, in the business context, a good reputation and repeat business. Wow! I must be good if people are calling me. While I had made great progress in caring for the neglected little girl, I knew that she was always in there and always wanting more love. Therefore, I could not trust myself without a plan.

- I had noticed that every time I said "yes" when I was ambivalent, I did not do very good work or enjoy it very much. So I had developed some self-talk that said, "While you are trying to decide, you are standing in the way of the perfect person getting this work, so get out of his or her way—and your way!"

- I definitely wanted to work less and enjoy it more. I wanted to grow my Midwest client base and not abandon my West Coast client base. I wanted to travel less. I wanted to shift my work gradually from "doing" to "enabling others to do."

- I developed a list of "yes" criteria, listed below in ranked order of importance:

  1. The work must be Twin Cities-based or somewhere to which I can travel there and back in one day.

  2. I will accept any work referred by Grove Consultants International (in San Francisco) that fits with the mix I want of training or consulting.

  3. I won't take any "one-night stands," that is, a one-off meeting that isn't tied to something larger.

  4. I will honor the "Aretha Rule," that is, my client and I will respect each other so we both do good work.

5. I must have expertise in the area requested or be willing to invest the time to get it.

6. I will travel to Europe, but generally not to Asia or South America.

7. I will take a job if I want to work with the person or company, even if it doesn't meet some of the above criteria. (Honor past relationships; keep repeat business where appropriate.)

Agreements with Myself

- I will keep an active list of first class "stand-ins" or referrals and follow up to see that they are a good substitute from the client's perspective.

- I will be willing to help the client find the right person.

- I will say "yes" to nothing on the spur of the moment. I'll wait until the next day to decide.

- I will build in the time to develop trust and respect in the relationship.

- I will feed my "keepers"—my past clients—to minimize the number of times I have to start from scratch. (*Note:* The result of this agreement is that, by 2000, eleven out of twenty-six consulting and training clients were new, so more than half were repeat business. I have grown my income substantially since 1996, but I have not been able to reduce the travel to where I want it to be.)

- I will monitor my activity so that I know where I am in congruence with my agreements.

- I will process the feelings that come up to grow my shifting internal wiring.

My Consulting Principles

- Be open to all the work in the system

- The work starts here

- Simple works

- Do excellent work

- Get out of your/their way

- Seed hope

- Be a friend

- Maintain confidentiality

- Provide fast turnaround on work

- Have fun doing serious work

- Remember that change hurts

⑥
Professional Work as an Opportunity for Personal Growth

Difficulty of Changing

As conscious consultants, we bring our whole selves forward when we engage with our clients in a process of change. Neither we nor our clients know exactly what will happen on the journey we jointly undertake. Because change is deeply challenging to anyone experiencing it, we can expect that difficulties will come up along the way—some that we anticipate and some that we do not. Although these difficulties may be uncomfortable, they offer us opportunities for real personal and professional growth.

You may have had the experience of deciding to change something in your life—and then finding that this decision and the actions that followed brought to light a number of other things that needed changing. It is like completely remodeling your kitchen. People who are veterans of major remodeling projects will tell you to count on delays and things going wrong—you can expect to cook on a hot plate and do dishes in the tub for longer than you thought! One way to work skillfully with this common experience is to assume that difficulty will come up along the way, so that when it does, you can say with humor and acceptance, "Oh, here is the problem. I was wondering when it would show up!"

An example from the world of consulting is when teams go through their development cycle and something happens that creates conflict—missed schedules, personality conflicts, unmet expectations, and so on. Knowing that "something" will happen in the middle of the process provides the opportunity to bring humor and compassion to the situation. "Oh, here we are in the middle of our team development and now we are having a crisis! Wow, we made it to the middle!"

Personal change is the same. We might think it will be easy and smooth, but inevitably something happens that makes it messy and tries our patience. Something catches us off guard and we revert to old behaviors. When this happens, we can consider it a valuable opportunity to discover something that will open the way for a new change project.

When we look deeply at what happens inside us in times of special difficulty, we can usually see two dynamics operating: *roadblocks* and *triggers*. We are often unconscious of them. If we bring awareness to them, we can develop new and more effective ways to respond, freeing ourselves from repeating unproductive patterns.

Roadblocks

A *roadblock* is an area within us where we carry unfinished business or old pain. The roadblock is with us all the time, and it repeats itself over and over. We are generally not conscious of the dynamic until it stops us. It takes some conscious work to find the root issue and to deal with it in a healthy way.

> I have a roadblock. It's the same thing, over and over. I always over-work and exhaust myself. I think I have to do all the work, and no one will help me. This has happened all of my life. No matter what the project or who my partners might be, this happens. As I have become more conscious, I have learned that I am not very easy to help. People may try, but I chase them off with a stick. Now I can see and feel myself when I do it, although I can't always stop myself. I realize now that I have this martyr thing going. I think it's about trying to prove that I am good. My family has the "never enough" disease, which means not only that I am never enough, but that no one else is ever enough either.
>
> While writing this book, I had the idea that I was working harder on it than my co-author Kristine was. Of course, I was getting exhausted, as usual,

and getting more and more annoyed. Like all good friends, we eventually had our fight. When it all came out, Kristine was annoyed with me because she thought she was working harder than I was! We both realized that we were experiencing the same roadblock at the same time on the same project. We took the opportunity to make a major change and helped each other a lot. I am on my way to curing my "never-enough" disease.

Renée M. Brown

Here is another example of a person becoming aware of a roadblock within himself.

"Scott" is an external consultant who explains, "For the last three years, I have been trying to be clear about and hold to my agreements with others. I expect people to keep their agreements. It seems like I keep hitting this issue a lot lately because my clients are not keeping their agreements. They cancel meetings, don't pay on time, or cancel the contract in midstream. I don't like how that makes me feel."

Scott worked with the steps of the Active Change Model in the following way to find his roadblock:

Perceive: *When an agreement is broken, I have a strong emotional reaction.*

Describe: *My reaction is usually one of anger and hurt.*

Accept: *I accept that I feel let down, pushed aside, and unimportant. I am also aware that I want to look at what I want to have happen over the long term. I understand that if someone does something and I get angry and stay angry, then I will be blocked in the relationship. If I want the relationship, then I can't carry the anger. The real effect of being in judgment is too high a price for me to pay: It means I cannot move forward.*

Question: *Scott developed these questions to help find his roadblock:*

- *Why do I set myself up with agreements that will be broken?*

- *Why is it so important to me that others live by their word?*

- *Do I break my own agreements?*

- *How do I expect others to react to me when I break my agreements?*

- *When was the last time I experienced someone breaking an agreement with me? What happened?*

- *When was a time earlier in my life that I experienced someone hurting me with a broken agreement?*

- *When was the earliest incident that I can remember when someone hurt me with a broken agreement? What was the outcome or consequence to me?*

It was this last question that helped Scott remember a time when he was in first grade and his mother was supposed to pick him up from school. She got tied up in a meeting and did not pick him up until 6:30 p.m. The school had closed, he was waiting outside, no one else was there, it was beginning to get dark, and it was bitterly cold. It was a terrifying experience for him. In describing this experience, Scott became aware that when someone says he or she will do something, Scott forms a strong emotional attachment to that agreement.

Act: With this knowledge, Scott decided to look at agreements with more flexibility and acceptance. "How people make agreements is their prerogative—it is the way they are and the way they operate. I cannot expect others to live up to my standard of agreements because they did not have the same childhood experience of being abandoned. So I am not going to expect that others will do as I do. With that I will have more freedom from expectations, and I won't be so hard on myself."

Foundation Development Plan: Scott also added this issue to his Foundation Development Plan. He decided to create a list of things he could do when people broke their agreements:

- *Journal, either through drawing or writing, what I am feeling about the broken agreement.*

- *Go for a long walk or get some other exercise and have a conversation with myself about how I am feeling.*

- *Sit in the hot tub until I am relaxed enough to take the next step.*

- *Ask myself how old I am feeling in this situation, and see whether I can find the roadblock experience.*

- *Ask myself what I am not getting, and then figure a way to get it for myself.*

By working through the Active Change Model and preparing his Foundation Development Plan, Scott ensured that change would happen in this area. The degree of change will depend on his commitment to his own growth.

We keep bumping up against our roadblocks until we consciously follow them back to their origin. When we see the source of our early wounds, we can move beyond the initial pain and be healthy again. The Active Change Model is our means to do this—bringing what is unconscious to the surface.

Triggers

Along with roadblocks, *triggers* have a large role in situations in which we experience great difficulty. A trigger is something that "sets us off." It touches parts of ourselves that carry an emotional charge from the past. Our reaction to a trigger will be to experience an inappropriate amount of emotion. The degree of our emotional response may seem reasonable to us, but to others it seems irrational. Triggers are sometimes referred to as "tracings" or "traumas."

> There are clues to "getting" myself that Bob Tannenbaum refers to as tracings. If I am in a conversation with someone, in a meeting, watching a TV show, or reading a book, I can notice an emotion arising inside of me and make note of it. I try to make connections between the situation that is currently happening and past events in my personal life (marriage, deaths, and so forth) where there was a similar emotion. When I can see the patterns in what I am noticing, I can ask, "Where did those come from?"
>
> Since one of my issues is around powerful authority figures, I can ask myself what I notice about my emotions and behaviors when I am having a conversation with such a person. What have I traced and noticed? I have discovered a few things and am getting a better understanding of my reaction in the moment, including how to set that aside and look at it with a third eye, asking myself, "Is this functional? Are the fears or hallucinations reasonable, or is something else impeding me? If this is not rational, do I have an opinion about the behavior? Am I able to set that aside and have a powerful relationship with powerful people?"
>
> *Chris Worley*

How do triggers operate? Life includes pain, and we create mechanisms to help us to avoid that pain. We engage in controlling, disconnecting, resisting, or other forms of avoidance behavior. Although we have the illusion that by creating walls we are protecting ourselves, we are actually becoming more rooted in pain. This causes us to unconsciously develop a habit of becoming numb to the pain. Then something happens that reconnects us to the locked-up pain—a trigger event. It pierces the unconscious, and suddenly the locked-up, numbed-out emotion flares out. Once it is out, we feel the emotion and are conscious of it, but we may not know where it came from or what to do about it.

Thinking we will be able to avoid triggers is another illusion. As long as we have old, unconscious, unfinished emotional pain, we will experience triggers. Once we acknowledge this, we can remind ourselves that triggers will come, and we can plan for how we can get out of the reaction mode and be a learner. Triggers help us to identify areas of personal health or dysfunction. When we have clarity about our triggers and how they operate, we can make conscious choices.

> These days I seem to have a huge emotional flare-up when someone tries to "tell" me what to do. I immediately become angry and go on the attack. I have started to realize that this is a big clue about a roadblock that I have, originating around how helpless I would feel when my father would tell me what to do. There were often big consequences for not following his rule, "When I say jump, you say 'how high'—on the way up." How it plays out is that someone will give me a suggestion, but it happens to be blunt and direct. I will hear it as an order and react as if I am hearing my father all over again, and I will unconsciously push back. I have avoided this in my work by being an external consultant, where I am being asked to enter as the "expert" and am not "told" what to do. But this darn issue finds other ways of sneaking in—in my personal life, my friendships, or even when writing this book! So I am aware there is a big issue around my father for me to work on, which may take years, but at least I am getting more aware of it when a trigger is touched off.
>
> *Kristine Quade*

Another awareness of a trigger might be experienced in this way:

> I know I am hitting a trigger when I start to "dis" someone else. The minute I start to feel defensive or make it "their fault," I know I need to stop and look at what's going on. I know I am trying to project something. My years of therapy have helped me to see that defensiveness reaction as a gift. I am able to ask myself, "Which of my sacred cows has been touched?" For me, it is usually competence. My head talk is, "If they just understood, they would know how right this is." If I complain about someone, it is a good sign for me to look

more deeply to understand the message. I ask myself, "Why is this bothering me so much?" It may be because we have different values, or it may be that I am judging that the person doesn't have enough integrity, courage, et cetera.

Jane Magruder Watkins

How Roadblocks and Triggers Impact Client Selection

In his book, *Boundaries and Relationships: Knowing, Protecting and Enjoying the Self*, Charles Whitfield (1993) says that we all have a deep desire to become whole and free, and that we choose or attract certain kinds of relationships that give us the opportunity to learn and to heal ourselves.

> My core assumption is that I am working as a consultant not to "help" other people, but, in fact, to continue my own inner work of self-differentiation. Although this sounds contradictory, given the fact that we typically define our role as helping others, I have come to see my purpose as self-focused, rather than other-focused. And oddly enough, when I lose sight of this purpose and think instead about how I can "help someone else," I find that I become more muddled and less effective in my role as a consultant.
>
> So, if I believe that the process of consulting is an opportunity for me to do my own inner work, I think my primary tasks are to become clearer about my own personal position in the world, to build my capacity to express my position clearly to my clients, and to remain calm and clear when my ideas or proposals are challenged. How am I with myself in relation to the person who has come to me with a problem or issue and is asking for assistance? When I work with clients, I find that, as long as I am committed to remaining clear, calm, and honest when expressing my ideas and perspective, then I find that my support is perceived as useful, and my projects and relationships tend to unfold successfully.
>
> *Peter Norlin*

If we draw relationships to us in order to heal ourselves, then we can count on the fact that all of our clients will bring that opportunity to us. We will draw clients who will trigger our roadblocks. When we identify what is going on in ourselves, we can get to the root of the roadblock and deal with it consciously.

> I have come to learn that the client who shows up for me is not simply a client, but also someone who comes with the gift of helping me discover a new

awareness about myself. I know that, in any client system, I am likely to experience some personal issue that I am working on. For instance, once I was facilitating a large group event. The attendees were employees of one company that had just merged with three others. The participants were resistant to hearing about where the organization was going as a result of this merger. They only wanted to know how they fit into the new company and what they would have to do to keep their jobs. They were angry with the CEO for not keeping them informed; they were feeling betrayed and feared the worst.

At the same time, I was just coming off a serious illness and was not feeling at my best. I was seriously questioning my competence and whether I had the stamina for a three-day event focused on creating a new culture. I feared the worst about my ability to keep up. I love doing large group events and wondered if I would be able to do this kind of work anymore because of my health. Would I need to find a new "passion" within my practice, and not do what I love anymore because I was not well enough? If I could not do work as intensively as before, what would I do, and how would I re-tool myself to do it?

I stopped on the afternoon of the second day to observe what was going on in the room and noticed that the participants were posing the same questions to each other that I was posing to myself. They were wondering about their ability to contribute to this new organization and whether they had what it took in context of what was needed for the future. It helped me to see my issue about contribution through my work.

Kristine Quade

Some individuals unconsciously select an organization to work with in order to work on a roadblock they have. Other individuals are drawn to particular organizations that appear to be places where they will be liked and appreciated, have their needs fulfilled, and find their desires nurtured and protected.

Planning for What May Happen

Certain things almost always happen in our work with clients, but when they arise, many consultants react as though they were unexpected. These reactions take a variety of forms. The consultant may go into panic mode when conflict surfaces; try to over-control the agenda; not pay attention to signals such as withdrawal; not utilize opportunities to reflect team member behaviors; or move the group or individual into a new activity that is not in sync with proper timing. Understanding what problems may arise during a consultation will help us to relax and to appreciate, utilize, or even possibly avoid unhealthy experiences. Here is a list of frequently encountered events, just so we can plan for them.

What Might Be Encountered in an Intervention

- People will fail to act at crucial points.
- Someone or everyone will resist.
- Someone will say something that annoys, inspires, or excites others.
- Interactions will get messy.
- Someone will make a mistake.
- When the work gets tough, someone will change his or her mind.
- Two agendas will be in play: the official one and the unofficial one.
- Everyone will have expectations, and they may all be different.
- Clients will be stretched during the work.
- Everyone will agree on the need for change but will disagree on what, how, or when.
- Some people will be physically present but not mentally present during the work.
- Along with the shared external conversations, there will be a private internal conversation in the mind of each team member.
- People will have differing perceptions about the value of the work.
- Some people will want the answer given to them.
- Most people will struggle for control, each in his or her own way.
- The work will unfold in its own cycle—like peeling an onion.
- Integrity will be tested.
- Everyone will have his or her own idea of what the truth is.
- There will be constraints or obstructions from outside.
- The work will foster connections with others.
- There will be a struggle to turn long hauls into short hauls.
- Individuals will engage in the task before they engage with one another.

- There will be a "hump"; sometimes we get over it and sometimes we get stuck.

- Politics will get in the way.

- Individuals will choose self-survival over organizational survival.

- There will be an awareness of having to "manage upward."

- People will be suspicious that the intervention is just the flavor of the month.

- People will hold back their energy until the way is clear.

- Clients will say or believe, "I can never reveal who I am in the organization because it will be used against me later."

- Change will take a lot of effort.

- Trust will be an issue.

- It will appear that people at the top can't make up their minds.

- Everyone and everything will have his or her own timing, and they may not be aligned.

- There will be a critical crisis that leads to a new level of operating.

- Just when things start moving, something will happen that derails the process.

- The rules of engagement will shift during the process.

- Fears will arise about the process, interactions, and relationships.

- Values will be different for everyone, and this will challenge personal interactions.

- Wisdom will come forward when people are present in both mind and body.

- If there is something that needs to happen, it will.

- Things will always be churning.

- People will want to be acknowledged for the talents they bring to the organization.

- Individuals will want to be heard and understood.

- We consultants will need to gulp before we take a risk.

- We will have feelings about the success of our work.

- We will find that success is tricky.

- Forgiveness will be a hard subject to approach.
- "Adapt or Die" will still be a relevant motto.
- Change will cause people to look deeply at themselves.
- Every change will bring about an equal and opposite counterforce.
- Each person will be committed to a goal to the extent that he or she participates in crafting it.
- Every group will have its own life force.
- Some or all of the people will be unhappy with the consultant.

When any of these show up as part of the individual and team process, they present opportunities for the consultant and client to interact in beneficial ways. For instance, the client might act out in such a way that we experience a trigger. If we can anticipate that this will happen, sooner or later, we can plan for it by using our Active Change Model and strengthening our Personal Foundations. It is the work at this level that will help us to be clear about our boundaries so that we can maintain them when the turmoil begins.

> When I facilitate a meeting or coach an individual, one thing that usually happens is that, periodically, people begin to feel a little overwhelmed with new thoughts, resistance, or whatever. Then they begin to "check out" and drift away from the process. I watch for this. I feel that this is a sign that everyone needs a little breather to balance out. It's not always a good idea to take a break, so what I do when this happens is tell a little story. The story I tell has to be related to our topic, but not too much, because it's really a little one- or two-minute vacation. I know clients think I am digressing when I do this—and I am—but quite deliberately. When my story is over, they are usually present again and ready to go; if not, I may tell another story, even more entertaining or off the point.
>
> Another thing to plan for is that frequently team members will break agreements they have made with each other. I know this will come, and I watch for it. I keep a running inventory of the group members, looking for their present mood, style, and timing. In particular, I know every situation calls for me to know what group members need *now* and how I need to speak so they will hear. For instance, when someone breaks a group agreement, I may:

- Only note it to myself, looking for an opportunity to raise the issue later, perhaps when the group's mood is more frustrated with the break-downs.

- Directly and immediately mention it, depending on the group's history and current need.

- Never mention it if this group seems to work best by direct experi-ence and not so well from feedback.

- Tell a story again, either right away or later. The story is usually a metaphor for what is happening, but it might be a story that is simi-lar to the event.

Over the years, I've invented many ways to respond to all of the things that usually happen. My clients get a custom job every time, and I am never bored.

Renée M. Brown

In this chapter, we have looked at how awareness of our roadblocks and trig-gers can help us change and heal ourselves. These patterns are not just happening *to* us—we may be unconsciously causing them to happen. Realizing that we attract particular clients into our practice to help us in our own healing will cause us to view our clients and their behavior as an opportunity for growth, rather than as another thing that keeps happening to us. By acknowledging and anticipating the many kinds of individual and group experiences that come up in interventions, we can plan for them and be prepared to help guide our clients through.

I think of roadblocks as empty holes and triggers as the land mines. My road-block is my continued development of my own voice. I grew up in a family with a dominant mom (whose siblings called her "General Patsy") and a pas-sive dad. I was the youngest in the family, with five older sisters. I was not usually picked to be first in the sports teams. I was not all that good at the dominant white male game or culture. Instead, as an introvert, I worked on listening, being a good witness, and studying human interaction.

I work with organizations to engage white men as full diversity partners. Most white males think of this as someone else's problem. Doing this work is an avenue for me to work on my self-issues. It is my opportunity to continue to learn and grow. I recognize that I had a controlling mom, and sometimes when I am around strong women I can be triggered. I also know that not being so caught up in the strong white male culture is an asset; it means I can help other white men realize they live in a white male "culture box" and that they can reclaim choices about who they are and who they want to be.

Kurt Hahn, the founder of Outward Bound, said, "Your disability is your opportunity." We need to learn how to use disabilities as assets. Growing up with strong, all-female influences and a less-than-assertive father has become my asset for the work that I do with white men.

Michael Welp

Using the Active Change Model

Waiting for an incredibly impressive list of strategies for dealing with the various scenarios that surface in our personal work or our work with clients? Working through these issues can actually be quite simple if we use the Active Change Model. The following example illustrates one way to apply the Active change Model.

Every once in a while, I will encounter an intervention that lacks the usual fun, creativity, and aliveness that I look for with clients. When I am able to stand back for a minute, I am usually able to see that I am working with a client without clear agreements. I may have been in a hurry when starting with the client or I may have been busy with other clients and was therefore inattentive to this one in the beginning. The result is that I get the feeling of being in a tug-of-war with the client. Things will slip by, what they said they would do is not getting done, communication will not be as crisp, people will miss meetings, and so on.

So I pause and reflect about what is going on, using the Active Change Model. Above, I have already Perceived, Described, and Accepted what is going on. Next, I move on to Question and Act.

Question: I start this process by listing questions. Whatever comes up, I write down, even if it does not make sense. Following is a sample list of questions and the answers that I came up with.

Q: What was going on with me during the startup with this client that distracted me from making clear agreements?

A: I was working with two other clients and totally juggling the calendar to fit in this particular client.

Q: What personal issues may have been distracting me?

A: I was worried that, if I did not take this client, when I finished the other work on the plate, there would not be a new client for me to shift to. I was worried about cash flow for the fall bills. Ah—I am in a new relationship and if I stay home, I may have to connect with my issues around intimacy! If I am working hard, I don't have time for the relationship and he will either understand or go away! (Here I found the nugget of what was really going on!)

Q: On a personal level, what sort of nonfunctioning agreements was I making with myself at the time I started with this client?

A: I am not able to say no to others who need help. I am not worth waiting for (both with clients and personally).

Q: What else do I want to say to myself?

A: If you believe that you are not worth waiting for, what is that doing to you on a physical, emotional, and spiritual basis?

Q: Where do you suppose that comes from in your history? What pattern (roadblock?) is coming up for you that you now have an opportunity to break?

Act: At this point, I decide to do a journaling exercise to expand the previous step and to find my agreements. Sometimes I use my left hand to write an agreement and my right hand to write what might get in the way. Or I might use two different color pens, one for questions and one for answers, so that I can slow down my brain enough to capture what is really going on. The net result is an awareness that it is about time I dealt with my intimacy issues. So off to my support group I go and begin to work a very old issue. I usually complete this process by writing out a 3″ x 5″ card and taping it to my bathroom mirror so I can see it morning and night. It will contain a list of questions or the new agreements I have made with myself, such as the following:

- In what ways *will* I be in my heart today? (asked in the morning)

- In what ways *was* I in my heart today? (asked in the evening)

- Don't make a decision right away; say, "I need to think about it."

- Listen with such passion that I can "feel" what the other person is saying.

- Note how each interaction changes the way I perceive the world.

I begin to experience my change process right away because I am now aware of how the intimacy issues are creeping into other places. I begin to drive more slowly and notice where I am going. I begin to turn off my cell phone and not answer my home phone after 4:00. I begin to schedule a "date" with my significant other and practice listening with the passion of "discovering who he is." Funny thing, I notice that I am now getting work with clients that is more fun and creative, and I feel really alive again.

Kristine Quade

Final Thoughts

At an International OD Congress in Mexico, a question was posed to Dr. Ezequiel Nieto Cardoso, the founding father of OD in Mexico and a master practitioner: "How do we justify charging so much for our services?" Ezequiel, suffering from Parkinson's disease, halted a minute to gain his equilibrium before replying in a halting voice:

"We *are* the tool. We are the *only* tool that we bring to the client system. If we allow ourselves to become rusty, to ignore our worth and our strength, then we have nothing of value to offer our clients."

7

Stories from the Field

Illustrating the Concepts

In order to help with the application of the concepts that have been presented in this book, we have selected five stories from practitioners in the field. Each has a different approach to the use of the material. Each story is rich with unique perspectives and application. These stories are intended to raise consciousness and to help you think about ways to strengthen your Personal Foundations.

Application of the Active Change Model
Kathy Joyce

This is the story of two directors and their twenty-three managers in a large West Coast company charged with merging the leadership staffs of two departments and downsizing appropriately. Simultaneously, two other locations were working through similar change efforts, and I acted as the facilitator for their process. At the end of a rigorous process, they made a courageous decision: The best business solution was to reduce their own ranks by 80 percent and move to self-managed teams. The story unfolds using the Active Change Model as follows:

Perceive

At the time the managers went offsite to examine their own staff structure, the change process had been underway among their employees and in their work areas for more than a year. Indications were that one department would be able to reduce the average work shift from thirty low-skilled employees on simple tasks to four or five skilled individuals on complex machines. In the other department, changes in schedules, loading, dispatching, and delivery had reduced the amount of work to a fraction of its pre-change level.

Describe

A group consisting of all managers from both departments worked together to create wall-sized work flow charts. They covered the charts with plastic, hung them in the break room and provided grease pencils and sticky notes to encourage employees to comment or make notations on the plastic flow charts. In the best spirit of "inclusion precludes exclusion and builds buy-in," they urged people to study the charts and indicate missing or underrepresented steps or tasks.

The anonymous comments were incorporated into the flow charts and taken to an offsite meeting. One employee note set the tone for the offsite to set staffing and supervision levels. This note was kept in its original form and posted on the board for the opening of the offsite session. The note said simply, "We used to take two hundred items to two hundred locations. Now one driver takes 50,000 items to one location. How much supervision does that take?!" It was, of course, a very good question and made it obvious that employees, as well as managers, were looking for an answer.

Accept

Having thoroughly quantified and mapped the "old process," the offsite began with professed commitments from both directors to ensure that core processes were covered in the revised structure. It took several more half-day sessions and another offsite session as the manager team wrestled with the new process flow, set production and machine parameters, and built and staffed shifts. At the end of each meeting, flip charts were posted in the break room.

Question

Armed with the most powerful data possible—every phase of the work they "supervised"—the directors and the managers sat down to design their future. The approach was to define success and map answers to the question, "What will make success possible?" Success was defined as having the product at the customer's door on time, in excellent condition, and with quality of content and presentation that precluded complaints.

The leadership group first produced a high-level, "30,000-foot" flow chart from production through delivery and then began defining the supervision required to ensure each step. Defining the leadership role in the pre-production steps went smoothly, but the group became stuck when looking at the part of the process for final production. The speed and efficiency of the new production process required the machine operators to problem solve and make decisions as they worked.

After struggling to define the role of supervision for the production run, the group took a different tack. They moved to the customer point of "success" and created a reverse process flow from the customer back into the organization, asking the same question at each step: "What makes that possible?" Again the work went smoothly until they reached the production phase. In frustration, the group stared at hours worth of work until one manager said, "If we've done everything right before production and we do everything right after production, there isn't a supervision role when we're running—the operators make the decisions." The insight was profound and was the cathartic moment in this process.

Act

Based on the truth blazoned in the flow chart, which had been validated by the work on shift and staff needs, this group of leaders acknowledged that there would be a minimal role for supervisors on future production runs. The recommendation delivered by this group of leaders was a true measure of commitment and vision. Implicit in their recommendation was that their traditional power base and probably their salaries and maybe their jobs would be eliminated. But, recommend they did. Their actions not only answered the question of what the new leadership structure would be but defined what it would take to ensure success in this new world. The recommendation included the need for specialized training on self-managed teams, problem solving, process improvement, and data collection. This group worked with those from the other two locations to create a road map to the newly visualized future state.

Change

All three locations developed a joint approach and successfully implemented retraining, a buyout, downsizing, and a restructuring, and they did so with no loss in production efficiency. The best measure of success, however, is that some managers chose to accept a demotion and stay to help the transition. Most of those people were still employed a year after the change—an even greater testament to the power of helping people see the full potential of change.

Application of the Personal Foundations
Chris Worley

I had been asked to work with an organization that had developed a good vision statement and wanted my help translating it into what the organization should look like in three years. Strategically, they wanted to move from the seventh largest firm in the industry to the number two position—a tall order for a commodity metals business. The group I was working with consisted of line managers, union representatives, technical people, and human resource representatives.

In preparation for a traditional action-planning meeting, I had interviewed people about how to move from where they were into the future. We were looking for key activities and trying to sequence them for the next two to three years.

As the meeting unfolded, a lot of data about what needed to happen was put on the table. My role was to facilitate and encourage. After some time, my observation was that the group was stuck over questions about the sequence and timing of these different events. In particular, it occurred to me that there was one event through which everything flowed and that the group was not seeing it.

I went to the board and drew the event in the middle and connected other activities to it (either before or after it in time). The drawing was a PERT chart from project management techniques. There were a number of activities that could happen before this one event, but nothing could happen after it until the event itself was conducted. The action of going to the board and making this issue visible changed the whole context of the conversation.

As I worked with the group, all of my ten Personal Foundations were operating. Here is what was happening with me during that process.

Identity

Much of the conversation concerned technical aspects of the business, and I understood only a limited set of the terminology. Internally, I kept asking myself, "How can I help these people solve these technical problems?" I consider myself a reasonably intelligent person who picks things up quickly, but this was a world I knew little about. It challenged my identity because an important conversation was taking place in the life of this group, but it was about something I didn't understand. Staying with the conversation and keeping it moving was hard, and clearly it was getting stalled. In retrospect, it had nothing to do with the business or project management and everything to do with my having this internal conversation about "who am I?"

Agreements

This was a fascinating assignment for me because of the alignment among the group members about how to treat each other. There was also good alignment between their views and my own; I was in alignment with them in the same way they wanted to be in alignment with each other.

Integrity

Integrity was a big value for them. If they felt that I was not making a contribution the way I could or that they were not pushing themselves the way they should, they would name it.

Authenticity

This was an interesting group of people. They were physical laborers with long family traditions with this company. Their grandparents had worked there, their parents had worked there, and they expected that their children might work there. They had strong feelings, emotions, and perspectives about their work, family, and community. They cared deeply about each other and the organization. If there was any "b.s." floating around, they called it. There was good alignment with what I would like to see and what they were in fact doing. I felt I could show up authentically in the organization and that was OK because that is how they were trying to show up.

Courage

Courage for them was in trying to push the envelope of what was possible in a mature commodities business. For example, the union had hired a temporary worker to come in and record the conversations and oral history of the project. She had been working for about six weeks or so when, toward the end of one of the meetings, someone asked her, "What do you see happening? What are your impressions of what we are trying to do?" She responded, "I have to tell you, this is the strangest thing I have ever seen. This is the first time I have ever been in an organization full of men where they are laughing, crying, yelling, and hugging." Although it was something the group thought it knew about itself, it was still good validation for them that they were attempting to accomplish something unique and risky.

Chris Argyris says that relationships are strongest when it is OK to discuss the undiscussables. As soon as I began to understand that this group was willing to talk, I began to show up in meetings, make suggestions, engage them in debate, and demonstrate courage. As soon as that happened, the relationships began to accelerate and gain urgency.

Timing

I felt it was critical for me to go to the board and draw the picture. I was worried about how to contribute to the conversation because of its technical nature, but when I suspended the worry, which took timing, knowledge, and wisdom, I was able to see that what they were struggling with was really a project management issue. From their point of view, I pulled something out of the hat and showed them how important the single event was. But for me, it was "duh!" For them it opened up the skies and put them on a different path. They began to understand the critical nature and relationships between events. In retrospect, my application of knowledge and timing was not so very brilliant, but it was powerful for them. The intuitive part of me saw and heard conversations about activities and in the middle was this little event or conference. No one seemed to notice that it was a demarking event and that things before and after flowed through it.

Knowledge

Suspension of my inner voice and my concerns over my worthiness allowed me to see and access a different kind of knowledge that was helpful to them. Setting aside the self-talk allowed me to see what was helpful. This was challenging to me because most of the conversation concerned technical issues. It was not something that I could help them with. The more chaotic the meeting became, with group members voicing additional ideas and making efforts to convince each other about the right way to go, the more I could see the data on the table differently. That was when I suspended what I was saying to myself.

Epilogue

This organization was later acquired, not the strategic route they originally had intended, but it fulfilled their goal nonetheless. I still receive e-mails from them that remind me of the time when I did the intervention. It did not seem like that big of a deal, but it did have an impact.

When I step back, I can see that there were powerful, knowledgeable, authority figures in this organization. Here was a culture in which I was expected to deal with authority in an authentic way. Yet I still struggle in my relationships with authority and wonder whether I am good enough.

I have begun to look for engagements that, for whatever reason, challenge this part of me. I believe that personal growth begins with a desire to understand issues, their nuances, layers, depth, source, and history. So I started working more intentionally on the issue of power and authority; I try to take work that exposes me to experts and high-level executives.

I am convinced that the better I understand my strengths, the better I understand my weaknesses and the dark sides of who I am, and the better I understand how I am in relationship with people, the more powerful I am as a consultant. My work is with groups wrestling with strategic issues on the one hand and team dynamics on the other. Power, authority, profit, norms, competition, and interpersonal relationships are all juxtaposed. The more I understand my own pre-dispositions with respect to conflict, authority, and not being good enough, the less likely I am to intervene with the client to serve my own needs. I stop intervening to make myself feel better and start to help clients to meet their objectives and to learn to do all of this work themselves. I am creating ownership, and I am doing a better job of transferring the skills and knowledge of management change to the client.

Foundational Development Based on Experience
Robert "Jake" Jacobs

I'd like to start this story by describing my present business and life circumstances, then return to a significant early professional experience, before finally concluding with a more recent application of lessons I've learned along the way.

For the past six months, I have been working with a strategic coach to support the transformation of my business and personal life—in a sense gaining the same benefits of accelerated and sustained change I offer my own clients. As part of this process, I have come to recognize that I am at my best when I am fully present. And part of being fully present, ironically for me, is not being too well-prepared. In my work with clients, having solutions on the front end works to my (and our) disadvantage.

I believe society in general values "doing our homework." And there are certain benefits to being prepared—more time for reflection, considered strategic decisions, more efficient use of time and resources. However, as the old adage goes, there can be too much of a good thing. Over-focusing on "getting ready" can lead to never "being ready," never achieving that clear, authentic side of being present and responsive in real time to the issues and opportunities I face in my life and work every day. Striking the right balance between these two is the key to my best work and my best life.

Early in my career, one of the first clients I worked with was "George" ("General George" to people in his organization, given his preferred management style). In this particular engagement, I was working with fifty or sixty people on a three-day event aimed at reaching new agreements about how different departments could best work together. Everything seemed to be progressing smoothly until the afternoon of the third day, when I introduced one of the last tasks needed to gain these agreements. Thinking I had done a good job in this introduction, I looked around the room only to realize that there was dead silence. No one was working. No agreements were being reached.

As I quickly scanned my mind regarding all that I knew at the time about facilitation techniques, it occurred to me that I had just entered uncharted waters. I had no answers for a situation I had never faced before. I decided against repeating the same instructions again, only louder (tempting though it may have been). I also determined that saying something to ease the tension would take the group's focus off the real issues that they were now facing.

So I stood there, thinking and hoping that something would shift in the group's dynamics. But nothing did. Finally, with a calm conviction, I decided to let this group know what I was thinking: "It's not important to me that you do what I just asked. I may not have asked you to do the right task. It is important that you do what you need to do, work that is important to you in reaching these agreements."

I summoned my courage, as the very real possibility loomed before us of these three days suddenly falling off the tracks irretrievably. I asked the group, "What do you want?" Without even looking in his direction, I could sense the frustration building in my client, "General George."

As if it happened yesterday, I can still recall the brave soul's voice from the back of the room call out at that moment, "I want a Diet Coke!" I thought to myself, "Well, there is a place to start at least" and replied, "Okay, you should go get one."

What I witnessed next was as much a minor miracle as it was predictable. Every person in the room immediately turned his or her chair toward the table and began very focused, energetic conversations.

No sooner had I exhaled with a sigh of relief than General George was at my side, red-faced and exhibiting all the signs of frustration and saying, "What is going on here? What are they talking about?!" Having little time to savor my recent triumph at having helped navigate our way through a critical choice point in the design, I responded honestly and innocently, "I have no idea what they are talking about!" George countered, "If you don't know what they are talking about, it could be anything . . . not even the right thing. Then what's the purpose of this event in the first place?" At that moment I recalled the purpose of the event: To have the group members come to agreements about how they could work better together. So I said, "I don't know what they are talking about, but I do know that this is the best that they have worked together during the three days of this event and probably for the last six months. So this must be a good start on that purpose."

George stepped back, took a look around the room, and said, "I can live with that for now." Throughout the rest of that afternoon, the group worked in new ways with each other, ultimately arriving at a set of agreements—taking a different path than we envisioned, but achieving the same outcomes.

The lesson I took away from that afternoon is one that I carry today: Although preparation is an important element of success, creating space for people to do the work they most need to do is an equally critical contribution that I can make to any group's evolution. I find that when I have the confidence and conviction that the group can and will do important and challenging work, at some level that seems to help them actually do this work.

Throughout my career, I have prepared materials, done my fair share of remote work getting prepared for client engagements, and stayed up more than my fair share of nights to make sure that things were in order for specific events. And don't get me wrong, this is all-important—but it is not the only part of the equation that is important. You see, as my business has expanded, I have found that some of these assumptions about what's required for success have been challenged. In retrospect, my level of preparation is not as critical and central as I always thought it was to the process. I can often add significant value by "just" being fully present. And sometimes being prepared actually gets in the way of being fully present.

Recently I was working in Indonesia on a global change effort with a health, environment, and safety organization. As part of a three-day meeting, we were strategizing about how to broaden the engagement most effectively to the entire organization by introducing a new management system that would enable people to operate more strategically, develop a more productive culture, and mitigate risks.

We had spent two and a half hours in the total group talking about what we should do next on the agenda. People from all over the world had devoted a significant chunk of time to planning their own next agenda item—with people becoming increasingly exasperated at this seemingly careless use of our precious time together. What the group was working were the same issues that the organization was dealing with on a daily basis. The conversation was about "What does the individual need? What does the whole group need? How do this meeting and the work we are doing fit with the progress being made by business units in different countries?" These different perspectives were playing out in this two-and-a-half-hour conversation just as they had played out in the larger organization for a number of years—and there was little collective progress to point to from our efforts.

It was at that point that I realized that our group's experience represented a fractal of the entire organization—a repeating pattern of part versus whole—and that any work we could do to break through this issue with this part of the system could lead to synergistic progress in the whole system. So I stopped the conversation and said, "If we better understood what is going on in this room, in this meeting, in this moment, it could help us to understand how to move the change effort forward in the whole system."

Up to that point, we had been working symptoms instead of understanding the deeper root causes underlying these symptoms. So I suggested that the group do a root cause analysis to see why we had been stuck in pain for so long dealing with the same issue. I asked them to understand aspects of the session that were working well and those that were getting in the way of progress. I told them that no one needed to use the same tool for their analysis, and they all chose a different approach that met their needs. They came up with powerful insights about why things were the way they were in the meeting and how to translate these lessons into the larger organization.

My learning was that this was the exact work that needed to be done, in the way that it needed to be done, and in the only setting in which it could be done. Wisdom is borne from experiences and principles that guide our lives and work. I knew I had been in a similar situation before, many years ago on the other side of the world with General George and his team, and I knew that the group's facing into these issues was a path that had truth. As Carlos Castaneda's mentor Don Juan has said, "When you come to a fork in the road ask, 'Which path is a path of truth?' and follow that path for it is a path of goodness."

And sometimes that path of truth is one on which I hear myself say, "I don't know." Not knowing, although at times an uncomfortable place to be, is also a place of great conversations and creativity. One of my unique abilities, which I am increasingly clear about, is in helping others be able to experience and then find their way through these places of "not knowing"—whether they are individuals, groups, or entire organizations. Peter Block has described this as helping people "step into their own vision of greatness."

As I pay more attention to how important it is for me to be present, I find that the same level of awareness begins to show up in my client organizations. In Indonesia it took two and a half hours to see what was "showing up" and to decide how in real time we could change our own experience and create our own future. Some of this I am confident we could chalk up to the group doing solid preparation work before the meeting so that we could engage with each other authentically when the opportunity arose. The remainder I am certain can be traced directly to the group choosing to be present and collectively taking full advantage of this opportunity. And within that delicate balancing act, I have come to believe, lies the key to better work and a better life.

Bringing the Inside Work to the Outside
Margaret Seidler

I have been an avid change agent for most of my work life. Yet only in the last several years have I begun to understand how my experiences, biases, and whatever else has occurred in my life impact my clients and their ability to succeed. I have also learned that a consultant's best intentions are insufficient when we are responsible for creating and implementing strategies that impact the lives of many others.

I've been working for the past three years as an internal consultant in one of the largest local government bodies in the United States. Taking any organization to greater heights of performance is difficult at best, and taking this organization forward in light of the political and entitlement environment has been more challenging and complex than my previous experiences.

As I came to know others and be known in the organization, I became the "next Coming," the person who could lead them to the brightness. One could also say I was just the latest hero. I was uncommonly accepted, hence excited and committed to making things better for all. My excitement was reflected in my pace and in my style. Over time, I learned my need for achievement distorted my view of where people were in their own ability to change.

As I led a group of senior managers in using the Malcolm Baldrige quality framework to improve their own departmental leadership, I was discouraged by their lack of speed. The urgency or need for change, while articulated, wasn't compelling. Proposals and plans were offered and discussed and modified, and discussed, and modified, and so on. Only months into the work did I suspect that their journey might be just one more way to keep busy as the clock continued to tick toward their retirement. Yes, we made progress, albeit slowly. I was frustrated, and they felt pushed. My work had turned into an internal consultant's worst nightmare, "Margaret's Project."

Consequently, I began to spend some time reflecting on how my perceptions and feelings impacted the group. As I began to see and accept what was really going on around me, I could see a group extremely dependent on me. I had helped to create just the opposite of what I wanted for them! Instead of learning and growing, they were looking to me for most of the answers. They weren't just keeping busy; they were dependent!

Drastic times call for drastic actions. I realized that removing myself as "leader" could quell internal resistance and place the ownership where changes could be made, at the senior management level. Well, some six months later, after I moved on to another part of the organization, it's working; the senior managers *are* making progress. They are now taking the leadership role that I envisioned from the start.

The further I get away from this situation, the more clearly and objectively I can see it. I had taken my clients to a place based on my own experiences, biases, and feelings. I had been unable to separate myself from my work. So I believe my personal work is to create the ability to see clearly and objectively in the present, to be a "conscious consultant." In order to do that, I have to separate my own perceptions and feelings from the group's work. The more I can do this, the more helpful I can be to the organizations I serve.

A Way of Being in a Consulting Relationship
Peter Norlin

Since I have found that certain organizing principles seem to surface in all work that I do, my approach to the process of consulting and working with organizations is now mobilized around four key dynamics: change, power, help, and learning.

I also believe that, at its core, the process of consulting requires that I work primarily and consciously on my own self-differentiation. I now believe that, as a consultant, my primary tasks are to become clearer about my own personal position in the world, to build my capacity to express my position clearly to my customers, and to remain calm and clear when my ideas or proposals are challenged. This is the basic, interior assumption that I now have about my practice.

So now I define the real purpose of "consulting" as an opportunity to do my own inner work. How am I *with myself* in relation to the person who has come to me with a problem or issue and who is asking for assistance? When I work with people, I find that as long as I am committed to remaining clear, calm, and honest when expressing my ideas and perspective to my customers, my support is perceived as useful, and my projects and relationships tend to unfold successfully. In the moment, I try to follow three crisp, but challenging behavioral guidelines: show up, tell the truth, and keep agreements.

All these internal commitments were challenged recently during a year-long project with a state government system, where I had been invited to be in conversation with the commissioner. His stated intention was to redesign the governance and service delivery structures of his entire organization in order to achieve a state mandate to provide service to the customers at the closest point of contact.

I initially recommended that he charter an integrated design team, consisting of a microcosm of the overall system, and that this team create a draft of the proposed redesign that would then go out for further review and input. I recommended that this team hold a three-day work conference, using a fast-cycle redesign process, to develop this first draft. Initially, this process seemed palatable to the commissioner and, with his nod, I began to develop and implement the preliminary steps in the work plan.

However, as I began to act on this proposal and the process that I thought we had agreed to, I began to realize that the commissioner was moving forward with a different approach. He seemed to be acting on a much different set of assumptions about the process and, as far as I was concerned, the process that he began to implement was not what we had "really" agreed to do.

For instance, I soon discovered that, rather than chartering a design team with statewide membership to work as a unified group, the commissioner had decided to invite each of the three future geographical service regions to hold its own redesign conferences. First, he chartered three separate "design teams," consisting of all the members of the current leadership team in each region. He then proposed that I work with each of these three regional teams to facilitate the development of a separate proposal for a statewide governance and service delivery structure. In his model, each of the three teams was then to bring its proposal to a consolidated meeting where the members of the three design teams from across the state would work to reach consensus on a statewide structure. In essence, by chartering the current leadership group to be the "design team" for the consensus work, the commissioner had put the current power structure in charge of its own restructuring.

At this point, I had to determine what would be the impact of an open confrontation with the commissioner. I was at a choice point about whom I was going to serve. The commissioner was the identified, paying customer, but the larger system was in turbulence—and the ultimate "customer." Could I find an opportunity to influence the commissioner to see the larger behavioral implications of the clear, potent double messages that I felt he was sending? I felt that I needed to find a way to help him to "choose to see" that, while he was espousing inclusion, self-management, and cooperation, his approach was escalating anxiety in the system, especially among his senior leaders. I was also aware that his senior staff felt that he had already made key decisions about the ultimate redesigned structure, but that he was giving the impression that he was open to the design teams' recommendations. As a final issue, he was creating considerable confusion among design team members because he would publicly agree to a proposed plan and then later revise components of the plan.

My internal dialogue was noisy and confusing: "If I leave this now, I will be abandoning the system. Other consultants could come in, but they will have difficulty in picking up the project in the middle and retaining the trust and confidence of the entire system." That was not something that I could contemplate comfortably. I felt I needed to be honest and forthright in the moment about what I thought needed to happen.

When I finally met with the commissioner, I began by saying that I was trying to understand how we could rely on our agreements if he continued to modify them unilaterally as we went along. I said that I needed to have confidence and trust between us and that perhaps we needed to re-think our consulting relationship.

His immediate response was clear, and he was able to explain his position and why he had made the decisions he had made. He did not see how his actions had breached any agreements. He believed only that he had made an adjustment. He also reaffirmed his decision to move forward with the project, and he expressed confidence that I would be able to support the redesign effort and said that he hoped I would continue as the consultant to the process.

This conversation was a turbulent experience for me. I wondered whether I should be doing this job—and doing it this way? Was I compromising my integrity and taking the easy way out? Should I be helping him to understand that behavioral science principles were being violated? I also wondered what the outcome would be, given my uncertainty in the moment.

For me, the challenge was working with a leader who believed that he knew what principles should guide a change process, but whose behavior gave a different set of messages. And because the system was being dragged through the process because of a state mandate, I wanted to help these people stand for themselves. I wanted to be a person who could ask these questions, contain my own anxiety, *and* facilitate a process that would help them move toward the future they collectively chose.

This project went on for a year. We would have meetings every two or three months to share the work and the proposals developed by the three design teams. We would use these events to try to come to consensus, but in reality, they seemed to be designing a "new" structure that provided each leader a similar, familiar leadership role, rather than truly building a governance structure and service delivery system that offered new, innovative solutions to long-standing problems.

However, along the way something slowly did begin to happen. People began to think openly about the frustrating problems in the current system. People who had not worked together in the past due to functions, mindsets, and structure began to listen to one another with growing curiosity. There was a marked shift in energy, a different spirit of openness, and a willingness to listen to each other and to respond positively to different perspectives.

Finally, at last, a service delivery structure was determined and a new governance model was created. There were, in fact, key parts of the structure that were consistent across the state, and there were some options that were individually customized due to geographical needs. People also found new roles, some of which were different from what they had envisioned a year before.

I feel curious about the process now, and I can also see certain choice points. Although I made those choices with consciousness in the moment, many did not lead to the outcomes that I had anticipated. However, in the moment, I also responded to the invitation to stay in the middle of the swirl of anxious energy and not to go to sleep, to flee, or to allow my own uncertainty to rise to a point at which I became dysfunctional.

In this situation, I believed that if I could hold the whole system with the clarity of my intention, I would be able to facilitate a process the client could use to redesign the system. If my intention was to hold what was messy and confusing, then they could breathe calmly enough to do "good enough" work and achieve useful results. In many ways, this experience exemplified what I find both thrilling and daunting about the work of process change. And in the process of this change, two of my own inner edges were exposed and sharpened, I believe.

First, I was required to relinquish my effort to go forward in the "right way" and instead was forced to go in another direction. Because I had put an internal stake in the ground about behavioral science "principles," I then had to decide whether, given the decision that the client had made, I could continue to work in this situation with integrity. At every step, I made my decisions with as much mindfulness as I could sustain, with as much integrity as I could muster, and with as much resolve as I could summon.

And at every step I struggled to let go of my assumption that I alone knew the "right way" to do the work. I also struggled to contain my internal concern that if these leaders did not follow my proposals, I might lose my *own* commitment to the process. As a consequence of this inner turmoil, I learned to stay light on my feet, to not sink into my own sense of lethargy or confusion, and to look for unexpected opportunities for influence in the moment. I came to "know" something else that seemed "right": If I was paying relentless attention to what was going on in the system moment-by-moment, then correct behavioral science principles would somehow show up in the activity I spontaneously created for the *next* moment.

Second, I believe that I was dealing with my own internal struggle around speaking the truth to a powerful person and then letting go and accepting the consequences. I had never before worked with a customer whose leadership style was more personally challenging.

In order to talk to the person who was in power and who did not have much tolerance for differences of opinion—the commissioner—I had to do my best to stay calm, to manage my own anxiety, and to make "I" statements clearly. I knew that I ran the risk of making him so angry with me that he might discount me and shove me further aside or simply not involve me further in the project.

As I took more risks to speak my own truth, I noticed that my relationship with the commissioner was shifting. I found that, as I pressed him less often for feedback or to reconfirm our agreements, he gradually began to initiate contact with me between formally arranged meetings. It appeared that he experienced a shift in his assessment of my value and in his perception of my commitment to him and to the system. I can only speculate about what specific dynamics caused this shift, but he became more spontaneous and relaxed during conversations and, over time, I found that he seemed more willing to disclose his own questions and uncertainty about the project. He also began to solicit my input about difficult decisions he was facing and to invite my suggestions about what strategies he might use to reach certain key objectives.

As I step back to reflect on this relationship, I believe that I took a risk to push back my self-fulfilling prophecy around power: When two opposing forces meet, only one person "wins." By holding onto my commitment to my own self-differentiation, I found a powerful, alternative message: "If I step fully into my own power, I will inevitably confront another's power. To maintain my power in that relationship, I must maintain integrity with my humility." This particular customer was an ideal mirror and an ideal teacher for this moment.

Concluding Thoughts

We hope that, in each of these stories, there has been a nugget of application that can be used either with the Active Change Model or in the strengthening of Personal Foundations. We are keenly aware that working this material is a never-ending process, as is all change. Our gift to the work of individual and organization change is that of our own consciousness. *We cannot hurry it, circumvent it, or control it. We can only join in and participate in the journey with our clients. That is the plan!*

Bibliography

Argyris, C. (1962). *Interpersonal competence in organizational effectiveness.* Homewood, IL: Dorsey Press.

Argyris, C. (1970). *Intervention theory and method.* Reading, MA: Addison-Wesley.

Argyris, C. (1993). *Knowledge for action: A guide to overcoming barriers to organizational change.* San Francisco, CA: Jossey-Bass.

Argyris, C. (1999). *Flawed advice and the management trap: How managers can know when they're getting good advice and when they're not.* New York: Oxford University Press.

Axelrod, R.H. (2000). *Terms of engagement: Changing the way we change organizations.* San Francisco, CA: Berrett-Koehler.

Beckhard, R. (1969). *Organization development: Strategies and models.* Reading, MA: Addison-Wesley.

Bellman, G.M. (1990). *The consultant's calling: Bringing who you are to what you do.* San Francisco, CA: Jossey-Bass.

Bellman, G.M. (1996). *Your signature path.* San Francisco, CA: Berrett-Koehler.

Bennis, W. (1993). *An invented life: Reflections on leadership and change.* Reading, MA: Addison-Wesley.

Blake, R.R, & Mouton, J.S. (1976). *Consultation.* Reading, MA: Addison-Wesley.

Block, P. (1981). *Flawless consulting.* San Francisco, CA: Jossey-Bass/Pfeiffer.

Block, P. (1987). *The empowered manager: Positive political skills at work.* San Francisco, CA: Jossey-Bass.

Block, P. (1993). *Stewardship: Choosing service over self-interest.* San Francisco, CA: Berrett-Koehler.

Block, P. (2000). *Flawless consulting* (2nd ed.). San Francisco, CA: Jossey-Bass/Pfeiffer.

Bridges, W. (1997). *Creating you & co.: Learn to think like the CEO of your own career.* Reading, MA: Addison-Wesley.

Carter-Scott, C. (2000). *If success is a game, these are the rules: Ten rules for a fulfilling life.* New York: Broadway Books.

Dannemiller Tyson Associates, Inc. (1990). *Interactive strategic planning: A consultant's guide.* Ann Arbor, MI: Author.

Drexler, A., Sibbett, D., & Forrester, R. (1988). *Team building: Blueprints for productivity and satisfaction.* Alexandria, VA: NTL Institute/San Francisco, CA: Jossey-Bass/Pfeiffer.

Dyer, W. (1977). *Team building: Issues and alternatives.* Reading, MA: Addison-Wesley.

Ford, D. (1998). *The dark side of the light chasers: Reclaiming your power, creativity, brilliance, and dreams.* New York: Riverhead Books.

Frankl, V. (1984). *Man's search for meaning.* New York: Simon & Schuster.

Freedman, A., & Zackrison, R. (2001). *Finding your way in the consulting jungle: A guidebook for organization development practitioners.* San Francisco, CA: Jossey-Bass/Pfeiffer.

French, W., & Bell, C., Jr. (1990). *Organization development: Behavioral science interventions for organizational improvement* (4th ed.). Upper Saddle River, NJ: Prentice-Hall.

Fritz, R. (1991). *Creating: A guide to the creative process.* New York: Ballantine.

Funches, D. (1989). Three gifts of the organization development practitioner. In W. Sikes, A. Drexler, & J. Gant (Eds.), *The emerging practice of organization development*. Alexandria, VA: NTL Institute.

Gray, J. (1999). *How to get what you want and want what you have.* New York: HarperCollins.

Kotter, J. (1996). *Leading change.* Boston, MA: Harvard Business School Press.

Lewin, K. (1958). Group decision and social change. In E.E. Maccoby, T.M. Newcomb, & E.L. Hartley (Eds.), *Readings in social psychology* (pp. 197–211). New York: Holt, Rinehart & Winston.

Lippitt, G., Langseth, P., & Mossop, J. (1991). *Implementing organizational change.* San Francisco, CA: Jossey-Bass.

Lippitt, G., & Lippitt, R. (1986). *The consulting process in action.* San Francisco, CA: Jossey-Bass/Pfeiffer.

May, R. (1983). *The discovery of being.* New York: W.W. Norton.

Nadler, D. (1977). *Feedback and organizational development: Using data based methods.* Reading, MA: Addison-Wesley.

Rogers, C. (1980). *A way of being.* New York: Houghton Mifflin.

Rothwell, B., Sullivan, R., & McLean G. (1995). *Practicing OD: A consultant's guide.* San Francisco, CA: Jossey-Bass/Pfeiffer.

Ruiz, D.M. (1997). *The four agreements: Wisdom book.* San Rafael, CA: Amber-Allen Publishing.

Schein, E.H. (1988). *Process consultation, volume I: Its roles in organization development* (rev. ed.). Reading, MA: Addison-Wesley.

Schein, E.H. (1999). *Process consultation revisited: Building the helping relationship.* Reading, MA: Addison-Wesley/Longman.

Seashore, C.N., Seashore, E.W., & Weinberg, G.M. (1991). *What did you say? The art of giving and receiving feedback.* North Attleborough, MA: Douglas Charles Press.

Steele, F. (1975). *Consulting for organizational change.* Amherst, MA: University of Massachusetts Press.

Terry, R.W. (1993). *Authentic leadership: Courage in action.* San Francisco, CA: Jossey-Bass.

Weisbord. M.R. (1978). *Organizational diagnosis: A workbook of theory and practice.* Reading, MA: Addison-Wesley.

Weisbord, M.R. (1993). *Discovering common ground: How future search conferences bring people together to achieve breakthrough innovation, empowerment, shared vision, and collaborative action.* San Francisco, CA: Berrett-Koehler.

Wilber, K. (1977). *The spectrum of consciousness.* Wheaton, IL: Quest Books.

Wheatley, M.J., & Kellner-Rogers, M. (1996). *A simpler way.* San Francisco, CA: Berrett-Koehler.

Whitfield, C. (1993). *Boundaries and relationships: Knowing, protecting and enjoying the self.* Deerfield Beach, FL: Health Communications.

Whitmore, J. (1996). *Coaching for performance: People skills for professionals.* London, England: Nicholas Brealey.

About the Authors

Kristine Quade brings her passion for conscious, healthy change to her work in large systems change with a proven international track record in mergers, culture change, strategic leadership alignment, process improvement, new company start-ups, and community development.

With over two hundred varied client system interventions, Ms. Quade has substantial expertise in building internal capacity for change. She has facilitated over eighteen thousand individuals in large group change efforts in the past six years. Ms Quade's clients experience her work as authentic, breakthrough, creative, flexible, transformative, and with quickly felt, measurable results.

Ms. Quade is an editor of the *Practicing Organization Development* Series. She has a commitment to advance the theory and practice of OD, provide access to leading-edge practices and applications, and help provide leadership for the redefinition of the field of organization development.

Renée **M. Brown** has worked in the field of individual, group, and organizational change for twenty-one years. Her work has focused on coaching, team building, and large group interventions. She is an expert on the dynamics of change and how people, groups, and organizations achieve it. Her coaching clients have included professionals from most fields, including many OD consultants who desire to deepen their personal change work. She is deeply committed to helping others to integrate change as a way of living.

Ms. Brown has developed a unique process that includes how to recognize unconscious sabotage, transform conflict into creativity, create healthy boundaries and agreements, discover and strengthen personal identity, and more. These techniques are practical applications that work to expand client awareness, promote change, and improve individual creativity, problem solving, and general balance in the real world. Her clients enjoy custom-tailored work that ranges from the corporate setting to adventure travel, and from individuals to large groups.

The authors can be reached at *www.consciousconsultant.com* or *www.quantum changeassociates.com*.

About the Editors

William J. Rothwell, Ph.D.,** is professor of human resource development in the College of Education at The Pennsylvania State University, University Park. He is also president of Rothwell and Associates, a private consulting firm that specializes in a broad array of organization development, human resource development, performance consulting, and human resource management services.

Dr. Rothwell has authored, co-authored, edited, or co-edited numerous publications, including *Practicing Organization Development* (with R. Sullivan and G. McLean, Jossey-Bass/Pfeiffer, 1995). Dr. Rothwell's latest publications include *The ASTD Reference Guide to Workplace Learning and Performance,* 3rd ed., 2 vols. (with H. Sredi, HRD Press, 2000); *The Competency Toolkit,* 2 vols. (with D. Dubois, HRD Press, 2000); *Human Performance Improvement: Building Practitioner Competence* (with C. Hohne and S. King, Gulf Publishing, 2000); *The Complete Guide to Training Delivery: A Competency-Based*

Approach (with S. King and M. King, Amacom, 2000); *Building In-House Leadership and Management Development Programs* (with H. Kazanas, Quorum Books, 1999); *The Action Learning Guidebook* (Jossey-Bass/Pfeiffer, 1999); and *Mastering the Instructional Design Process,* 2nd ed. (with H. Kazanas, Jossey-Bass/Pfeiffer, 1998).

Dr. Rothwell's consulting client list includes thirty-two companies from the *Fortune* 500.

Roland Sullivan has worked as an organization development (OD) pioneer with nearly eight hundred organizations in ten countries and virtually every major industry.

Mr. Sullivan specializes in the science and art of systematic and systemic change, executive team building, and facilitating Whole System Transformation Conferences—large interactive meetings with from three hundred to fifteen hundred people.

Mr. Sullivan has taught courses in OD at seven universities, and his writings on OD have been widely published. With Dr. Rothwell and Dr. McLean, he was co-editor of *Practicing OD: A Consultant's Guide* (Jossey-Bass/Pfeiffer, 1995).

For over two decades, Mr. Sullivan has served as chair of the OD Institute's Committee to Define Knowledge and Skills for Competence in OD and was a recent recipient of the Outstanding OD Consultant of the World award from the OD Institute.

Mr. Sullivan's current professional learning is available at *www.RolandSullivan.com.*

Kristine Quade is an independent consultant who combines her background as an attorney with a master's degree in organization development from Pepperdine University, and years of experience as both an internal and external OD consultant.

Ms. Quade draws from experiences in guiding teams from divergent areas within corporations and across many levels of executives and employees. She has facilitated leadership alignment, culture change, support system alignment, quality process improvements, organizational redesign, and the creation of clear strategic intent that results in significant bottom-line results. A believer in whole systems change, she has developed the expertise to facilitate groups ranging in size from eight to two thousand in the same room for a three-day change process.

Recognized as the 1996 Minnesota Organization Development Practitioner of the Year, Ms. Quade teaches in the master's programs at Pepperdine University and the University of Minnesota at Mankato and the master's and doctoral programs at the University of St. Thomas in Minneapolis. She is a frequent presenter at the Organization Development National Conference and also at the International OD Congress and the International Association of Facilitators.

Index